DOES GOD MAKE RADIATORS?

DOES GOD MAKE RADIATORS?

Dispatches from the front line of fatherhood

Tim Lott

ISBN-13: 978-1494219666

Husbands never become good; they merely become proficient.
- H. L. Mencken

How do you answer questions from your children like 'When did people start?' and 'Does God Make Radiators'? What is the best way to annoy your wife? When did men stop being able to put up shelves? How do you face the death of a parent? Should husbands and wives stop sleeping together?

These and many other dilemmas of family life are touched on, but never solved, by Guardian columnist, novelist, broadcaster and aspiring husband and father, Tim Lott.

INTRODUCTION: THE
DISCOVERY OF WOMEN

Philip Larkin once suggested that arrival of children into a life was dilution rather than addition. He was wrong – but I can see his point. For, having accumulated four daughters, a wife and an ex-wife, I am a man, diluted.

Not a *person,* diluted, mind you. It is my masculinity that has been softened, pummeled, undermined and subverted. I am deeply glad that I had four daughters. I am happy for both my marriages. One of them, after 12 years of partnership, even survives, even, at times, appears to prosper.

But there is no doubt that the whole process has taken something away from me. So perhaps it is not even dilution, but subtraction. What have primarily been taken away are illusions. Illusions about what I think of as the three F's. – freedom, family and femaleness (which is not, I think, an elegant word, but comes less laden with baggage than 'femininity').

The inception of a family in the early 1990s pleasantly destroyed my illusions of freedom. I believed for much of my early life, like many young men, that freedom was the ultimate goal of life. To be untrammelled, unattached, a feather light mote of dust on the face of the earth was my fantasy– picking up and leaving jobs, women, places, friends, like gewgaws to be abandoned when I grew weary of them. Peter Fonda in 'Easy Rider' was the template, just as the

Dustin Hoffman's Benjamin Braddock in 'The Graduate' - his face falling into stony panic in the final frame as he stole away his bride - was the outcome at all costs to be avoided.

Having a family meant letting go of that callow dream – and the fact that I had never attained it in the first place did nothing to reduce its power. I thought I would mourn its loss, but being in a family suited me. It turned out that it was security, not isolation, that liberated you. With the solid structure of a family at my epicenter, I could find the mental resources to purse the lone life of a writer which I had always coveted, but barely dared to embrace.

So it was no coincidence that shortly after I married and started a family that I both started and finished my first, (still unpublished) novel. It thought of it as my third child - after my two daughters, who I shall call Jean, now 18, and Rose, now 16 (pseudonymed after their paternal grandmothers).

The sense of connection with my children was immense, and my happiness at being a father profound - but the dilemmas that family life threw up, while inevitable, seemed insoluble. For as the illusion of freedom was defeated, another was punctured – the illusion of the 'happy family'.

Whatever being part of a newly-minted family gave me, and it gave me much, I was forced to understand the deeply political nature of marriage – in the broadest sense. How it revolved around power, communication or the lack of it as a form of warfare, psychological self-preservation and much other that was never featured in the romcoms or the pages of Cosmopolitan.

Very soon I founds myself once again idealizing the freedom I had so recently eschewed, even as I continued to acknowledge that it was a lie. For life, while stable, was now all constriction and demand and negotiation and conflict.

I came to understand that women refused to conform to your myth of them in a marriage, just as men refuse to conform to women's myth of them as husbands. Also 'wives' and 'women', it turned out, were very different creatures.

(I use the word 'wife' at all times to delineate 'long term partner'. All that is required to belong to this club is deep familiarity and confinement in close proximity with someone you are in an intimate adult relationship with over an extended period of years)

The pressure of the gap between our expectations and the fractious reality turned out to be too great. Thus, after seven years, I found myself cast into state of 'freedom' again. It turned out - surprise – that I liked it no more than the first time round. So, predictably, I tried again. I remarried and had two more daughters - 'Eva' (now 9) and 'Louise' (now 5). The constriction, the demand, the negotiation and conflict, all resumed – as did the immense love to all my offspring.

The family home holds up magnifying mirrors to the personality. All the vertices of the human soul are writ large within those private parameters, where there is no social convention to restrain them – only reward and punishment and whatever reserves of grace that happen to be gifted to each individual.

So much for family. So much for freedom. As for femaleness, my attitude has transformed beyond recognition during my life. I grew up with two brothers in a pre-feminist era (I was born in pre-feminist 1956). My attitude to women, probably up until my late 20's - I know now - was entirely based on misunderstanding, willful or not.

I did not believe that women were either virgins or whores, although I did think there were girls (they were all 'girls' then) that 'did 'and girls that 'didn't' and I much coveted the former. But I did have a set of inherited beliefs that were – in my very early days of dating, in working class suburbia circa late 1970's – more or less axiomatic to my place and time.

These beliefs were as follows: that women were morally better than men – I would have used the word 'nicer'. They didn't like sport or music very much and they were unduly fascinated by personal relationships. They were much more committed to doing their homework and behaving themselves than boys. They took fewer risks. They were less willing to engage in sex without some form of bargain being struck. In short, they were admirable, but a bit stuffy.

That was the limit of what I believed to be my knowledge, other than the fact that, along with most men of my class and generation, I saw women almost entirely as sex objects. That is to say, what I required mainly from women was mainly that they would be prepared to enter into some variety of sexual congress with me and that the attributes or otherwise of their respective personalities came very much secondary to this consideration.

The rest of the stuff – conversation, walking hand in hand by the river, going to soppy crap movies like 'Love Story' was a necessary tithe you had to pay in order to get laid – or jerked off, or whatever was attainable. It was a retrograde and immature attitude - of course. It was also that attitude of just about every young man from my background at that time, and, thank god, the continuing spread of feminism has done much to marginalise, though not completely eliminate, such a wide-of-the mark perspective.

Thirty years later, like most of my generation, I stand corrected and a number of fronts. Women are not nicer then men. Neither are they boring. Neither are they purely there to satisfy my sexual fantasies. They are women – in all their variety. They do not come in one mould.

And yet, and yet – I am sure there is something that links the female sex together. The only trouble is, I'm not sure what it is. I could suggest a few tropes – female solidarity, for instance, which in the face of male intractability or even hostility is a fact.

There is also, I think, a facility for cunning and the prioritisation of the emotional life over the coldly rational as a guide for action. There is also a certain ruthlessness of will that has the power to defeat most men in the long run. And given the continuing popularity of women's magazines, many women appear to be still fascinated by the minutiae of personal relationships. It is this last element that I share with them – which is probably why, on the whole, I get on pretty well with women (bearing in mind, always, the division between women and wives).

Such is my 'take' on women, anyway (and every man has one, and it is usually different from what they tell women it is). Daughters are slightly different. They are what you might call incipient women. My four daughters are still being poured into whatever mould they will eventually come to fill. Thus they are, for the time being at least, 'my children' rather than 'members of the opposite sex'.

They have personality characteristics that are not, I think, 'gendered' (although the younger ones remain stubbornly fond of fluffy animals). 'Jean' is volatile, witty and emotional. 'Rose' centered and serene. 'Eva' is the most unfortunate inheritor of most of my more daunting personality traits - absent-minded, forgetful, impractical and half in a daydream. 'Louise' is volatile, witty and emotional. Thus we come full circle.

While we are on the subject of nomenclature and personality, my wife, wishes for the purposes of this column, to be known as 'my wife' - even though she objects to the 'my', it sounds less disrespectful than 'the'. She is a highly intelligent (a university lecturer in English), a strong feminist, ambitious, combative, and largely dismissive of my talents, abilities and potential. She thinks, in short, that I am an idiot. She is thus well qualified to have earned the soubriquet of 'wife'.

Why has she agreed to me writing this weekly column? This leads me to the next thing I Know About Women – that they are deeply pragmatic. She agreed because of the money it will bring to the family. She wants the things that wives typically covet – a stress free loft conversion, a husband who listens to her with full attention on all matters however unengaging, point the brickwork at the same time and complete seven other impossible tasks before breakfast. I spend much of my time trying and failing to give her those things and receive scant credit for the effort. But that, again, is the nature of wives.

In conclusion, what is this column going to be about? I am not sure. My whole life has been an exercise in 'winging it' and this is no exception. Certainly at its heart will be family life and children, and of course, the interplay between men and women. That interface between two opposing poles or modes of life, like the nodes of an electrical connection – both as different as can be, but necessary to complete the circuit of family life.

it is only a single perspective, obviously – the perspective of one, who in the words of an African letterist - forwarded to me on the Internet - who is 'a very much bewifed and childrenised gentleman'.

How I love ring of that phrase, 'bewifed and childrenised'. And the fact that this letter was written in 1929 says something about the constancy of the challenges of familial relationships. As for honesty – well, I will be as honest as I can, but honesty, like all things in family life, is bound to be compromised in the service of propriety or of kindness.

My wife always likes to say, when I catch her out in some occasional petty deception (my prejudice is that women, or at any rate, wives, are generally more 'economical with the actualite' then men) that 'the truth is overrated.'

I do not agree – but I do believe that the truth must always be partial, and in a public column like this, inevitably self censored, watered down, if you will. Nevertheless, things diluted, *pace* Larkin, can still retain a great fascination, I am sure. They can certainly be more easily swallowed without choking, and I have no intention of being 'provocative' or controversial for its own sake. But I will tell it as plain as I can. God knows, I suspect that's going to get me into trouble enough.

PICASSO VS. DROPPED PIZZA

My wife and I have taken a long time to get round to visiting Ripley's Believe it Or Not in Piccadilly Circus. Not because it's expensive - which it is. It's probably because it's a bit vulgar.

The V&A, it's not. It has a lot of pointless sculptures made of matchsticks. Primarily it features freaks – the man with a) the biggest nose in history b) only a torso c) two pupils in each eye.

It's brilliant. My nine year old loved it. This is the same girl who groans every time we take her to a 'real' museum. She detects the whiff of self-improvement from twenty paces, and takes a similar attitude to art galleries. All she wants to do is stay at home watch the Simpsons. And read books, which we don't have to nag her to do, because she loves them.

But we don't let her slob about too much, even reading. We want our children to be cultured. They go to French lessons, learn piano, attend art classes. There was the ballet phase. And the yoga. We are not content with them being children. We want them to be paragons, advertisements for ourselves. We're not content with Polly Pocket. We want Polymath and Polyglot.

I am perhaps less concerned with producing an incipient Renaissance adult than my wife. If she leans towards the Helicopter Parent end of the spectrum, I lurch toward the Submarine end – present, yet mostly invisible.

I have a view of developmental psychology, which is not popular with my wife (who I admire greatly and genuinely for her unstinting efforts). This can be summed up as It Will All Come Out in The Wash. Children's propensities cannot be drummed into them. They can only be allowed to emerge.

This is not just the theory of someone who is a lazy feckless arse (which is pretty much sums up my wife's position). Stephen Pinker's classic book 'The Blank Slate' produces compelling evidence showing that parents, outside of outright abuse and neglect, have little influence on the outcomes of children's personalities and proclivities. Genes count for a lot, and so do peer groups. But the parents? Practically nil.

Counter intuitive? Probably. Terrifying? Definitely. Because if Pinker is right, we have virtually no power to nurture our children's cultural (or any other sort of) sensitivities. Our efforts to transform their inner clay into bone china are doomed.

My view is Pinkerite. What will be will be. Ease off the pressure cooker. Let them be bored sometimes– what the writer Michael Chabon calls 'The Satori of Boredom'. You don't need to speak French (if you're serious, try Mandarin Chinese). Your child isn't going to be a ballet dancer. And they can't be taught why an early Picasso is more aesthetically satisfying than a dropped pizza.

I am informed by the fact that my childhood was a culture free zone, and yet I have a hunger for culture all my adult life. It was in me and it came out. The same is true of my wife, but she drew different conclusions – that her children weren't going to be as starved of the finer things, as she was. She is not wrong, and neither am I. She is ever the Yin to my Yang.

I am with my wife absolutely on one thing – reading to your children every night is a must, so long as they enjoy it. But children are not a project to be completed, they are the inhabitants of childhood, a magical realm where they will never visit again.

Let them live there, nurtured, protected and reasonably unharassed, and they will grow fully into themselves. Loafing about, a touch of junk TV, a peanut butter sandwich, a comic, Ripley's - we should not shy away from such a childhood despite our high-minded imprecations. Childhood is not a series of achievements to be displayed like trophies. It's meant to be fun – believe it or not.

THE LAST HANDYMAN

There is one single factor that has been responsible, in my view, more than any other for the shrinking of men's status in women's eyes over the last few generations. It is not our lack of emotional intelligence, or our inability to multi task. Men have lost ground for a simple reason. They can no longer put up a decent shelf.

Time was when the idea of a man in his shed whittling away interminably at some geeky household project was considered an imprimatur of naffness. But how many women now secretly long for that shed, that spirit level, that deftness with a plane?

I once used to try and be handy around the house. I put up shelves above my both elder children's beds. They fell down. I hung pictures on the wall. They fell off. I topped up the oil in the car. In the windscreen washer reservoir. Things I glued together, after having broken them, fell apart. The inanimate world has long convinced me of the hopelessness of challenging its innate hostility.

My wife would like to believe that this was a very specific and individual idiocy on my part, and that in this department most other men were as gods, but from my inquiries amongst contemporaries, such practical skills, once such a central part of being a husband, are rarer than jam in a Tesco doughnut. The love affair between men, screwdrivers and Rawlplugs is over. A socket set is no more a welcome birthday gift for a man than a new saucepan for a woman.

This may seem a trivial loss, even a sort of progress. After all, many of us can afford to splash out on a handyman for an hour or two to free a sticky window jamb or paint a flaking frame. But symbolically, it is a hard adjustment to make. My wife, at some level, still expects me to be able to do this stuff. It remains, in the back drawer of her soul, a mark of masculinity.

I would not go so far as to say that I agree with her. However, I do experience a certain nostalgia for a skill I never had, rather in the way Daily Mail readers experience a longing for a past that never was.

It's not quite the same thing, but last week I climbed up our garden tree to rescue our new kitten. I didn't drop the kitten and I didn't break the tree. It was quite the manliest thing I'd done for several years and my wife's face glowed as I carried her safely in my arms down the ladder (the kitten, not the wife).

This experience almost led me to pick up a DIY manual and start learning about how to make a dovetail joint snug or raise an RSJ, whatever that is. But then I remember why I'm not handy. It isn't only because I'm incompetent. It's because I really, really hate it.

Handiwork is rather like the gap between the delicious, bulging hamburger that Michael Douglas character in the film 'Falling Down' sees on the poster above the serving counter and the limp, soggy reality that he gets handed. The wall, when you finish painting it, is not as it appears on the tin or as it features in your imagination. The fence, when you have erected it, is not rugged but coarse and cheap looking. The kitchen, when you have installed it, bears only the faintest, pale resemblance to the gorgeous, glamorous one on the catalogue. It is all very dispiriting.

The death of the handyman, for me, goes unmourned. But like the passing of the man-as-soldier, and the man-as-provider, it leaves a thin film of nostalgia in the mouth, a faint false memory of the man I, and many of us, might have been, but never shall be. But it usually fades pretty quickly after I've spent 20 minutes mowing the lawn.

DIARY OF A SCHOOL MORNING

5.00 a.m. Wake up needing a piss. Worry about prostate cancer.

6.00 a.m. Cat comes into room. Starts scratching table leg with claws. Wife yells at cat. Cat leaves.

7.30 a.m. Switch on light to check time. Wife yells at me. Switch light off. Make note to get clock with illuminated dial.

7.45 a.m. Get up. Go into girls' bedroom. Pull up blind to wake girls up.

7.50 a.m. Wife goes into girls' bedroom. Pulls blind down again.

7.55 a.m. Go into girls' bedroom and switch light on. Make noise. Prod them. Wife accuses me of child abuse. Switches light off.

8.05 a.m. School gates close in 40 minutes. Children finally stir. I ask what they want for breakfast. Louise, 6, won't tell me. I tell her that in that case I'll make whatever I want and she'll have to eat it. I ask them to start getting dressed.

8.07 a.m. Make lunchboxes for Louise and Eva (10). Peanut butter sandwiches not allowed in case Louise waves it in the direction of someone with a nut allergy and gives them a seizure. Peanut butter is the only filling she will eat. Put salami in instead. Remember that she will only eat salami when not in sandwich. Remove salami. Make healthy jam sandwich for her instead. Ham one for Eva. Cut off crusts. Add rice cakes (no crisps allowed) and fruit (which they will not eat) and hard-boiled eggs (which they will not eat).

8.15 a.m. Breakfast ready. Return upstairs. Girls both still in pants.

Threaten to shout at them if they do not hurry up.

8.17 a.m. Shout at them. Both remark, casually, that they hate me.

8.19 a.m. Still partially dressed, they sit down for breakfast. Louise refuses what I prepared. I ask her what she wants. She won't tell me.

8.21 a.m. Eva has eaten her breakfast. Louise has been staring at hers for some time now. She claims I have no right to tell her what to do.

8.22 a.m. Still staring.

8.23 a.m. Still staring.

8.24 a.m. I feed her, complaining that I should not have to feed a six year old.

8.29 a.m. Louise still not ready. I begin to dress her, complaining that I shouldn't have to dress a six year old.

8.30 a.m. Eva can't find her shoes.

8.31 a.m. Louise can't find her shoes.

8.32 a.m. Louise pretends to brush teeth but only eats the toothpaste. I pretend not to notice.

8.33 a.m. Search of Eva's shoes abandoned. Louise's shoes found in garden under trampoline.

8.34 a.m. Try to brush Eva's hair. She screams. I give up. She tries to brush it herself. Looks like a birds nest. I Let it go.

8.35 a.m. Children inspect lunchboxes. Complain. I take the fruit out. And the eggs.

8.37 a.m. Eva can't find her satchel. Louise is complaining about her tights, which she says chafe her. I try to distract her.

8.39 a.m. Change Louise's tights. We leave. Six minutes to gates closing. Eva still searching for something or other in the house.

8.41 a.m. Louise moving very slowly in general direction of school. I suggest that she gets a move on. She picks up something filthy from the ground and inspects if for a minute or two.

8.43 a.m. Eva can be seen at the other end of the street moving in our direction.

8.45 a.m. School bell ringing to announce closing of gates. Several hundred yards to go.

8.47 a.m. Squeeze into playground as gates closing. Louise insists that I transfer contents of her lunchbox to a lunchbox she thinks is prettier. Believing this to be an unreasonable request, I decline. She tells me that she hates me. I say goodbye to Louise. She doesn't answer.

8.48 a.m. Outside school gates. Shake hands, kiss and hug other parents who have all, by the look on their faces, been through the same ordeal. 'See you again tomorrow' they say. 'Yeh' I say. 'Tomorrow.'

CHILDREN: AN APPRECIATION

After receiving feedback from my children that my column is too negative – "you're always *complaining*" – I have decided risk my reputation as a curmudgeon and compose a paean to family life.

This is against my principles. Such hagiography is usually covered by parenting magazines, romantic books and sentimental movies. But if anybody who reads this column doesn't have children, they might want to know why anybody bothers.

John Updike once said that the most beautiful sight a man will ever behold is a woman's naked body. He omitted the sight of a child's face. Such faces in the house, such exquisite moving portraits, every day they strike you with awe. The most sublime painting could never compete.

Children are funny. The fact that the humour is entirely unconscious adds to its value. If you haven't had children, think of the funniest comedian you've ever seen, and multiply the laughs by a factor of ten. That's how funny kids are. And you get free performances every day.

Their very first joke, trying to walk and falling over, never pales. And that's just the slapstick. It gets better when they acquire the power of speech. I would recount some examples, but family humour does not travel. Take it out of the home and it dies like a joke told by a computer.

When they're not making you laugh, they're laughing. Laughter rings throughout any house with children in it, and it is like HRT to older bones, renewing and refreshing and healing. Children love life in a way you have forgotten to, and they insist on reminding you.

Children can also be surprisingly wise – or at least they have a great talent for stating thing so obvious they feel profound. As Louise, my five year old said the other day, "I wish there was no such thing as dead. But if there wasn't, all the people would fall off the earth."

Famously, their most unique talent is that of Being Cute. One can never find an adult cute, and I'm not sure when this particular ability disappears, but as long as it lasts, it is golden.

Last week I looked through the front window of the house to see Louise alone, on her knees, eyes closed, repeatedly kissing our brand new kitten on the whiskers. I'm not a man much given to going 'aaaaaaah', but put a kitten next a kid and there aren't really any other responses available.

You can see now why I choose not to write celebrations of family life. It is difficult to do without being nauseating. Yet I must continue.

What is more joyful, safe and happy than to lie in bed with your partner and children in the morning before the day begins, the duvet a soft magical carapace against harm? What happiness can compare with the ecstasies of greed and delight on Christmases and birthdays? Is there a more gorgeously fabricated object on the earth than the child's lovingly crayoned and paint splattered greeting card?

I am sure you are beginning to pine for a whiff of acerbity, for a splash of vinegar, but I am resolved not to falter. So may I speak of the smell of children, that unmistakable perfume that you lose as you age, like innocence itself? And the power of children's love, that gushes, floods the rooms and the house and the air itself. Who else will run to you when you return home from work as if you were Jesus on the third day? Who else will look at you as if you never have, and never could, do anything wrong?

Children make you do things you would never do and feel things that you could never feel. They are life itself, concentrated, raw, untrammeled. Keep your singing whales, your soaring eagles, your noble lions, your heroes and Helens of Troy. A human child is the most beautiful thing in the universe.

MEMORIES OF FREEDOM

This week I stumbled across a blog called 'Things I Miss About Being Childless'. It listed spontaneity, unbridled intimacy, watching TV without having the channel changed, and being in the bathroom without an audience.

This appeared on a Baby Blog, so aimed at new parents, but as I inch towards my 60's, I too, begin to think fondly about the time when I had no children. This was also prompted by the fact that some of my friends are now enjoying, in retirement, that happy state of being where, once again, they can live for themselves with their offspring grown up and their pensions bearing fruit.

The thoughts can be tinged slightly with envy. I do not have a pension, and my when my six year old, Louise, is out of higher education I will be over 70. It seems a bit late for me to cruise around re-living my twenties in a sports car or taking a gap year in far-flung parts of the world.

I would not swap my children for any kind of liberty, but I remember, like a barely heard tune, the melody of being childless. One of the simplest pleasures - long gone - is to get up in the morning at exactly the time I want to. This is a treat now confined to my occasional lone forays to a writing retreat where I am reminded of how profoundly wonderful it is to lounge, guilt free, under the duvet with no prospect of being disturbed and no urgent tasks to complete.

The financial freedom of independence is likewise a faint memory. This is not to say I live my life in penury – I make sure to look after myself, having watched some of my friends suffer under the weight of their own belief in their 'responsibilities'. But the mental state whereby I only had myself to support or had no responsibility is as evanescent as the memory of my first girlfriend's perfume.

What else was good before children arrived? The relative emotional order. Children scatter themselves like exploded bombs – possessions, emotions, complaints, imprecations flying through the air and leaving a mess on the carpet. Peace of mind is hard to come by in the middle of a never-ending shitstorm.

Also long gone is calm, ordered adult relationships. . Couples without children do not really understand the gulf between being partners and being parents. Just the two of you means having to negotiate i.e. argue, occasionally, about what film you want to see or what kind of wine to buy. Being parents means negotiating every-thing, all the time, every day, and your plans always coming second to the kids.

But then again, now it comes back to me that there were things unappealing about being childless. The loneliness of oneself. The purposelessness of merely career. The egotistic absence of real, messy human connection. The long lie-ins because you couldn't be both-ered to get up and do something you didn't want to do enough to get up for.

The insistent demands to 'have fun' with your friends down the pub, or worse, a club, shouting endless nonsense across a soundscape loud music. The vanity of clothes shopping and the tiresomeness of keeping up with the news, fashion and 'culture' because you felt you had to, given all the time you had on your hands. Staring at incom-prehensible works of art and nodding sagely instead of admitting, as I would now, that you think they are shit.

Come to think of it, the time before children was a somewhat barren place, more attractive as a misty memory than as a lived real-ity. I suspect the same feeling might come over me when I do finally get to 70 – suddenly free to be bored again, and to do nothing whatsoever. My children will fade into adults, and I will fade into someone who used to have children. And my god, that I *will* feel nostalgic for.

HOW TO SLEEP TOGETHER

I am gradually, but remorselessly, being pushed out of the marital bedroom. The presence of six cats, four of them so small as to be easily squashed by a clumsy male foot is only the start of it.

My wife seems to have had her laptop computer grafted onto the end of her fingertips now, so that is always with her and always switched on which makes it hard for me to sleep, or in fact gain her uninterrupted attention, or any sort of attention at all. It is her real partner in life now, and that is a fact I have to face.

Furthermore, my wife – understandably – dislikes my snoring. Which is not unfair. Once, when I was sleeping in a tent on the pavement outside my local library in order to try and prevent it being closed by the council, a passer by asked another volunteer if there was an angry dog inside the tent. That is the general sonic tenor of the night noises I make.

My wife is constantly stealing the bedcovers while simultaneously accusing me of doing the same. She is a light sleeper - if I get up in the night to take a piss, she usually complains, making me feel guilty. Her hands and feet are horribly cold and she always tries to warm them up on my bare skin. And she often turns the light on when she comes to bed (she usually goes up after me) on the pretext of looking for something or other, usually her laptop.

This technological aspect is a big part of what I suspect is not only a personal by a societal sleep crisis – people have long had rows about whether they watch TV in bed, but now it's about texting and emailing and tweeting after hours. There's a lot going on in the bedroom, just what not used to go on when we were first married.

I love sleep, but I'm really not getting enough of it – or not enough of good enough quality. I know this because although I probably get at least eight hours a night, I am still tired come the afternoon, when I usually take a nap.

So it has been occurring to me of late. Why sleep together at all? Why not follow the Queen/Prince Philip way and keep a safe distance? Sleeping alone in a bed – on the rare occasions I manage to do it – is unquestionably marvelous. All that space and silence and non-wifeness. It's like peace.

There is a lot of evidence that sleeping apart is gathering popularity – at least in America, who the British tend to follow quite closely in terms of social trends. There, the National Association of House builders says its expects 60 per cent of custom homes to have dual master bedrooms by 2015. If this is anything like a guide to how many couples are sleeping together, then a trend is gathering momentum.

One 2005 American survey found that nearly one in four couples sleep in separate beds – mainly for the obvious reason that it gives them a better nights sleep. You might think that trading intimacy for 40 winks is a devil's bargain, suitable only for those whose marriages are heading for the rocks, but it's not necessarily that simple. Getting enough sleep is not merely about being tired, but general health.

A survey of 70,000 women over 16 years, published in 2005 showed that women who slept five or fewer hours a night were a third more likely to put on at least 33lbs than sound sleepers. That's a big difference. So, it appears, sleeping together, since it tends to result in disturbed sleep, makes you fat. The scientific explanation for this is that after just a few days of sleep restriction, the hormones that control appetite cause people to become hungrier. So women who slept less might eat more.

The effect of this weight effect on men is not known, which unfortunately deprives me of an excuse for my muffin tops. However, it does help explain why I can't remember people's names or get my birthday dates mixed up, because studies at the University of Vienna in 2006 showed that sharing a bed with a partner, for men specifically, reduces their brain power. They performed worse in cognitive tests than when they slept alone. Again, this was due to lack of sleep (for some reason it didn't affect the women in the same way). So unless something is done soon, we are going to end up with a generation of fat women living with stupid men.

The main British guru of sleep studies is Dr. Neil Stanley, who doesn't share a bed with his own wife. He is evangelical about the subject of separate beds. His studies suggest that on average, couples suffered more than 50 per cent more sleep disturbances if they shared a bed.

Sleep disturbance a big effect on health, with an increase in incidences of depression, stroke, heart disease and respiratory failure. It's also disproportionately correlated with divorce.

"Poor sleep is bad for your physical, mental and emotional health. There is no good thing about poor sleep," says Stanley. Thus sleep disturbance is not only about your partner kicking, stealing the bedclothes and waking you up in the night going to the loo. Stanley points out that the British average is to have a double bed of 4'6", whereas a standard single bed is 2'6" or 3'. "That means you have nine inches less sleeping space in your bed than your child does in theirs".

Stanley also pointed out that the habit of couples living in double beds was a relatively recent cultural development. People moved into double beds at the beginning of the industrial revolution, when families moved into cities and found themselves short of living space. In ancient Rome, the marital bed was a place for sex, but not for sleeping.

The idea that people should sleep together out of a desire for intimacy holds little appeal for Stanley – "Sleep is the most self-ish thing you can do. People say they like the feeling of having their partner next to them when they are asleep. But you have to be awake to feel that. We all know what its like to sleep in a bed with someone and have a cuddle. But at one point you say 'I'm going to sleep now. Why not at that point just take yourself down the landing?"

Why not indeed? However, for me, such a move would be a radical and somewhat disturbing experiment. Sleeping alone is for old couples and couples who have no physical interest in one another any more. The marital bed isn't just a sleeping arrangement. It represents closeness, sharing, the married state. Without a bed to climb in to together at the end of the day, are you really any more than two people under the same roof?

And yet – perhaps I am being too set in my ways. I shouldn't fool myself. I *am* old – a few years shy of 60. So why pretend that I am not? Why not behave like the codger I am clearly becoming? My wife wouldn't blink twice if I moved into the next room (she's not what you would call a needy sort of woman). It might even give our sex life a fillip – you know, creeping in to the other's room of a midnight hour and all that.

Yet I just can't quite get my head round it. Perhaps I am just sentimental. To lie in bed and touch your partner at night, even with a partner who has appendages as cold as frozen cod portions, is something you don't ever do with anyone else. To listen to their night noises, and experience their odours, however unsavory, likewise.

It is not always a pleasant experience to share a bed with some-one. But it is rather unique, and it sets the mark on the particular status of the married condition. And most couples continue to take this view – according to one survey, only 8 per cent of couples in their 40's and 50's sleep in separate rooms. The temptations does grow as you get older though – more than 40 percent of the over 70's sleep apart.

One family therapist put it this way - "the biggest problem in every couple is disconnection. And this decreases intimacy. It starts with I'm going to take this kid here you and can take the other one there." And sleeping alone means physical distance, which can lead to emotional distance. "A logical decision in one area has consequences in other areas"

As it happened, I spent the night before writing this column in the spare bed, and I must say I had a wonderful night's sleep. I could grunt and snort to my heart's delight, shuffle about under the covers and wander off to the loo when I felt like it without having to worry about someone silently cursing me.

I'm thinking a compromise may be in order – maybe weekends together and weekdays apart. But another part of me thinks it's the thin end of the wedge. And the thick end of a wedge is designed to put a lot of space between objects. Already separated by technology, we will be just two people living under the same roof. That may be a relationship of sorts. But it's not a marriage.

PINK STINKS – UP TO A POINT

It was my youngest daughters 6ᵗʰ birthday last week. Her gift haul included Lego Friends (Lego designed specifically for girls), 'My Little Pony' accessories, a fluffy bunny and a Minnie Mouse sweet-shop. She loved her presents, although they were obviously a moral disgrace, since they underwrote and perpetuated the patriarchy.

Or that, at least, is what one woman I spoke to, remarked when I was discussing the subject. The gifts were 'gendered'. So why don't I give a shit? (My wife doesn't care either "I'm not *that* kind of feminist").

What kind of feminist is that? I suppose one who takes it all a bit too far and a bit too earnestly. My wife's generation – she's in her early 40's – was brought up with even more pink fluffy iron-and-apron type objects than my daughters have been faced with, and it hasn't been any obstacle to producing the largest generation of more or less radicalised women in history. But some stuff just won't go away, and bunnies and ponies probably fall into that category.

The 'Pink Stinks' movement, I have full sympathy for, on aes-thetic grounds as much as political grounds. It appeals, I think, partly because it taps into something nascent. My third daughter held an 'I Hate Pink' party, unprompted, when she was 6, not out of feminist conviction but because of a spontaneous dislike of naffness. And that I think we can all sign up for.

I just happen to believe that the link between children's toys and adult behavior is quite hard to demonstrate. When I was growing up, there was only one thing I wanted to do, and that was shoot people. If you wanted to see a shy little boy rendered ecstatic, give him a toy gun. But I have had relatively little desire to go on a shooting spree as an adult.

Guns assuage boys feelings of helplessness, and that is a fantasy all children, both female and male, covet. The same woman who complained to me that these gifts were a moral disgrace, also pointed out that she thought fairies and princesses and any girl figure with a magical power were actually OK , because they made girls, in the same way, feel powerful.

Gendered toys, although regrettable, may not be such a terrible thing. The nuancing of these marketing strategies actually opens out possibilities. If Lego were all building trucks, factories and farms, girls would probably be not that interested in what is actually a very creative and hands on sort of toy. Sling in a few ponies and an array of little plastic girlfriends, and it was the first toy that both my youngest and her sister went for out of the pile on the birthday morning, and has kept them occupied every since.

It's really no different to providing Action Men dolls for little boys. Yes, they are dolls that ostensibly kill people (or other dolls). But at least they are dolls, and they get boys thinking in a different sort of way.

A lot of gendered toy marketing is pretty rank. At Christmas, my ten year old was given a Monopoly For Girls, which was indeed pink, and instead of normal properties had nail manicure salons and mobile phone cards. This really did stick in my craw. It didn't improve the game, it specifically excluded boys, and it was, in all, tacky and unnecessary, a pure act of profit maximization to a market sector.

You could say the same of Lego Friends I suppose. Perhaps it's just a matter of taste and degree – Lego Friends tweak the toy, but don't entirely subsume the concept in sexist stereotypes. Rather they use the fact – or construction, if you prefer - of femaleness to edge girls towards something they might traditionally eschew. But no girl, I suspect would turn against Monopoly because there wasn't enough pink. And therein lies the difference between cynical opportunism and pragmatic, even enlightened, marketing.

CAMPAIGN FOR REAL GODPARENTS

According to Wikipedia, a godparent is a 'an individual chosen by the parents to take an interest in the child's upbringing and personal development... and ensuring the child's religious education is carried out'.

Much as I hate to disagree with the oracle, this definition is flat wrong. Godparents are the friends of yours that have spare cash and who are most likely to dole out presents and folding money on special occasions.

On a less cynical interpretation, godparenthood seems mainly to be a gesture from the birth parents towards their best friends, a kind of symbolic – and free – gift, which has precious little to do with the child in question. On this definition, a request to be a godparent really says 'we really, really like you (at the moment) so here's this honorary title which you are at liberty to ignore completely'.

Both these manifestations of the modern godparent have little to do with its original meaning. No real duties are attached – unless, perhaps, both parents are killed in a car crash, in which case the godparents are meant to bring up the kids. But, hey, who's left to bitch about it if you dump them in an orphanage?

Time, I think, to start a campaign for Real Godparents - and I speak as a hopeless godparent myself. Only one of my friends has ever had the rashness to ask me to act in this role, and I have assiduously ignored my duties ever since.

Is it, perhaps, possible to go back to basics and that original Wiki-definition - an individual chosen by the parents to take an interest in the child's upbringing and personal and spiritual development.?

It would be tricky, I confess. If any of my children's' godparents started ringing me up and checking out that I was doing my job properly , sticking their nose into my parenting choices and whatever I deemed their appropriate personal development to be, I would take it pretty tardily. If they started nagging me about taking my kids to church, I might answer with some decidedly pagan adjectives.

However, that doesn't mean that godparents couldn't – in theory at least - be put to proper use. This would start with godparents not being chosen because they were your bestest friends, or because they were had the freest hands with the dough, but because they were wise. As godparents, they would be expected to bring that wisdom in some fashion to the child's life – either through the gifts of books, or experiences, or poems, or themselves, or anything they chose, so long as the end of enlightenment was the one being served.

I know this concept of 'wisdom' is an old fashioned one, but I happen to believe in it, and I do have friends whom I particularly value for having their heads screwed on right. In an ideal world, I would like those friends – if appointed godparents – to take their role seriously, but with unobtrusiveness.

This might mean that, on or around the birthdays of their godchildren they gave them not a cheque or a boxed DVD set of 'Glee', but took them out to – say - the theatre and offered them a few words of sage advice on being around on this planet and growing up in general.

A godparent could occupy a de facto safe place for a child to access – they could be someone who a child could turn to when matters were too sensitive to be brought before parents. As such, they might act as pro bono counsellors rather than fairy godparents or ATMs. In this, the original meaning of the word 'godparent' might start to reappear.

Of course, have no wish to impose my morals on other people. Therefore, I would like to emphasise, to all my children's godparents, that I recognize that high ideals are hard to achieve and even harder to maintain. In that event, cheques and gifts in kind will continue to be accepted. Thank you.

JUST GROW UP

Sooner or later as a parent, you are going to arrive at a moment when you turn to one of your children and utter the words you once swore to yourself you would never speak to your own children- 'just grow up'.

I can't remember when I started to tell my kids to grow up – or even more absurdly, to 'stop acting like a child' – but I am aware of the magnetic pull of the phrase.

The demand implies the question , 'why can't a child be more like an adult?' , i.e. rational, purposeful, prepared to play by the rules. I don't speak the words often, but the sentiment is always lurking – for instance, this week, when I found my six year old, with ten minutes to go before the school gates closed, lying on her back still dressed in her pants saying 'I just need some quiet time'.

At that moment, I wasn't amused, but looking back on it , if not funny, then at it's at least ironic. One treasures more than anything that special quality children have – childishness - and yet one is simultaneously engaged on a mission to destroy it.

It is the sad duty of parents to remove the golden dust of childhood, layer by layer, by insisting on the necessities of life – by imparting the knowledge that narcissism, however charming, has to be leavened by concern for others, that arrangements once made must be kept to (including school), that certain spontaneous behaviours, like dropping your knickers and showing everyone in the church your bum while giggling hysterically, are not, in the long run acceptable.

Again ironically, it was a common trope of my generation to refuse to grow up. The idea was to stay young forever – to be spontaneous, sexy, juvenile, partygoing, exhibitionist and wild for a long as possible. This principle certainly seems to have continued for many well into parenthood. Why, after all, should the children have all the fun?

I am fairly atypical in that I have actually always wanted to grow up – even when I was very young. To be a man rather than a boy seemed to be a worthy goal – to acquire dignity, wisdom, a measured, perhaps even Olympian view of life. I didn't want to be thrown around by emotions in the service of 'spontaneity'. I didn't want to be selfish, or defined by my peer group. I thought from a very early age that being grown up was a goal worth aiming for.

Yet the process of having children yourself ultimately divests you of the hope of ever really reaching maturity. What children and adults, faced with each other, both experience is a feeling of intense helplessness – and this results, in both cases, in tantrums, squabbles, and mild emotional violence. To have children is to realize that the child inside you is never going to go away, to understand that the raw vulnerability that children experience is only ever managed or buried, not eliminated.

The quality of being grown up is something that doesn't necessarily come with age – although it seems to be born within some people. I am frequently nonplussed by the equilibrium which my ten year old frequently displays when punished or yelled at. In the first case she is wont to openly admit that the punishment was her proper due, and take it without complaint. In the second case, she will disdain the childishness of her parents with a resigned and magnanimous shrug, as if that kind of behavior is only to be expected from adults.

In fact she would be entirely justified in telling us to start 'acting our age' would it not almost certainly both set us off on another round of tantrums at her precocity. And the saddest thing is that we probably really are acting our age – that in some ways, our age never changes, however much the flesh ripes and rots.

WOMEN ARE GUILTY

I was a guest on BBC Women's Hour the other week, and one of the contributors made an interesting remark – an unusual event in itself for WH, but this comment actually got me thinking.

She said, "I don't know any woman who doesn't suffer from guilt'. I have no way of knowing whether or not this is true, but it feels plausible. There is for a modern woman plenty they can find to feel guilty about. Perhaps the food binge, the shopping splurge, the career woman struggling with maternal guilt. Perhaps the failure of yet another diet, the collapse of another exercise regime, the malicious comment later regretted.

I have rarely come across a man tormented by everyday guilt. Perhaps they just keep it quiet. Either way, guilt is a pernicious business that destroys more than it creates. But no one can ever quite say what it is, which is probably why it is so difficult to shake off.

It is frequently confused with conscience. Conscience is 'good' guilt - recognising that you have done something wrong, atoning or apologizing for it, and then moving on. Guilt is stickier than this. It seems to find a semi-permanent niche in the psyche of those who are susceptible to it.

People who are inclined to feelings of guilt – i.e. feeling bad when they have done nothing in particular wrong – come as several types. There are those who felt as children that they were Bad and are spending the rest of their lives flailing their arms trying to keep this perception at bay. These are the Damaged Guilty. They include people who were mistreated or neglected in some fashion.

Then there are the Ideological Guilty – those whose beliefs about how virtuous themselves and other people should be should be are unrealistically elevated. The Ideologically Guilty believe that people should be pure, good and beyond reproach. They feel endlessly disappointed with themselves - and other people - when they are confronted with the fact that the default human condition is weakness and flaw. Women, with their cultural patriarchal legacy of being Madonnas (as an alternative to Whores) seem to me particularly susceptible to this variety of guilt.

This kind of guilt is largely self-directed, but some people inflict guilt on others to make them miserable – the Guilt Dispensers. The Jewish Mother is the classic stereotype for this, but it tends to apply in closely-knit families generally. In marriages, Guilt Dispensers often pair up with the Damaged Guilty, thus setting up a power dynamic, with the GD inevitably having the upper hand over the DG.

Guilt can make you behave atrociously – not only towards yourself but towards others. Quite apart from those who work to make other people feel guilty, there are those who punish others in order to evade their own feelings of guilt.

Nevertheless, there are those – the church for instance, and the political establishment – who think we couldn't do without guilt. In this view guilt is a necessary corrective to hedge against bad or anti social behavior.

I disagree. Marriages and families would certainly be better without it (which is not to say they would be better without conscience). My personal theory about guilt is that appears in proportion to the amount of freewill you think you have, because guilty people think they are responsible for everything. It is a form of control freakery.

I have come to the conclusion that one of a husband's subtlest and most difficult task is to save their wives from guilt. This usually means being determined to head of their culturally inherited self-sacrificing Madonna-like instincts, and not offering, but *insisting,* that you organize the holiday/pick up the kids/clean the house/ insert unpleasant task here. Being given no choice in the matter saves the oppression of guilt – and it saves you from the punishment that guilt can so often elicit. I recommend it. One of these days, I might even try it.

HOMEWORK SUCKS

Something I share with my childhood self is a profound dislike of homework. I reluctantly submitted to its inevitability as a child but as an adult I resent it, both on the part of myself and my own children.

My six-year-old sitting down to homework at the weekend is merely academic tokenism. She already spends six and a half an hour a day at school – why should she have to do more? My ten year old has been complaining about her weekend burden for years – quite rightly.

Why do we torment our kids in this way? I had no homework during my primary school years and very little during the first years of grammar school. This was the norm in the 1960s and '70s. . At some point since, the work 'ethic' that has infected national life generally – not that it's particularly ethical – insists that if you're not working, you're doing something faintly dissolute or purposeless, even if you're six.

Nothing is more precious than those islands of childhood that are left untouched by invading adults and their fund of schemes for the future when you finally make it as a Worthy Citizen. Let children drift and dream and make up games with plastic guns and My Little Pony, watch unsuitable TV and stare out the window. But this makes evangelists for the work society uneasy.

Homework is unnecessary. The 2006 book 'The Case Against Homework' by Sarah Bennet and Nancy Kalish, points out that "all the credible research on homework suggests that for younger kids, homework has *no connection with positive learning outcomes,* (my italics) and for older kids, the benefits of homework level off sharply after the first couple assignments."

Homework generates conflict. There is the, 'have you done your homework yet' row, which is repeated every weekend, with the parents taking on the role of reluctant Gradgrinds. There is the 'where is your homework?' row in the mornings.

Worse still, parents are required to help. But most parents are not trained teachers. They are often impatient and ineffective. When I 'help' my own children, I have certain, unreasonable, expectations of them. When they are unable to do what I consider to be simple, I get annoyed. I am never more likely to lose my temper with my children than during a homework session.

This is upsetting all round, and worse still, it works against creating a love of learning in childhood – which for me is what education is all about. Study becomes associated in the young mind with conflict and unhappiness.

Furthermore, as my ten year old points out, why should children have to go through this when adults don't? Yes, in some jobs – notably teaching – work has to be brought home. But in many jobs, when you're finished, you're finished. Come the end of the day, your work is done. Friday night, you have 60 clear hours in which to unwind and refresh yourself.

But for children, starting very young, the extra curricular work just gets more and more intense at the same time as you face the poignancy of your childhood slowly running out of road. It's like a dismal, ever more insistent herald of things to come.

Since the progressive teaching of the 1970s was rejected – to some extent, with good reason - we have slipped back into Victorian models of education. I am reminded of that moral failure, Heinrich Hoffman's 'Johnny Head in Air' who, daydreaming, fell in the river and nearly drowned. This served as a warning to any child who spent too much time indulging his or her imagination.

Johnny should have been paying attention, ideally with his head buried in a dry piece of homework. My preferred template is Richmal Crompton's William Brown – carefree, up to no good, with plenty of time to pleasurably kill. That's the difference a real childhood and one that is simply training for life as a drone.

DREAM HOUSES

Since the title of this column is 'Man about the House' I have decided it's time this man wrote a column about the house.

What is a house? Obviously, a roof and four walls, if you want to be reductionist about it. But it is also a theatre – the most vivid showpiece for all our materialist fantasies. And a money pit. And, above all, an arena of combat.

This is a subject much on my mind at the moment, because my wife and I are preparing to acquire that essential accouterment of the middle class (along with the Stukke chair and the sash windows) the Loft Conversion. My wife has been trying to persuade me for the last eight years that we 'need' one. Everyone else in the bloody street seems to have one. Finally, I have crumbled like a reclaimed brick.

Interestingly, one of my most recurrent dreams in my life is that of undiscovered spaces in my home. Sometimes, deep in slumber, I will walk through a door and be confronted by a whole new and beautiful land that I had never hitherto noticed.

These images, a dream analyst told me once, were dreams of freedom. And yet with my rational mind, I tend to understand the enlarging of our house as a dream of constriction – simply because we're both going to have to work harder to pay for it.

I admit - I am worried. I dislike dealing with workmen, since, lacking technical knowledge, I am always on the back foot. I am rendered anxious by the way the budget always goes far higher than it was meant to. And I am discomfited by the way the work is rarely as good as it should have been given the astronomical cost of improving it. Yes, the house will increase in value – but at the same time we will have to pay interest every month on a much larger loan, so how much value is added is a moot point.

At the same time, I have to admit that I've begun to work up a bit of excitement about the prospect. A whole new floor! A special eyrie to which we can retreat! Yet the neurotic in me keeps whispering questions. Where are we going put all the stuff we had in the loft before it was converted? In the bins, no doubt, where it should have been put long ago. Or not.

Plenty of room for conflict there, as we both indulge in separate fantasies that something or other that hasn't been used for five years will somehow get used in the next decade. A cheap printer with the lead missing, a faulty microcassette transcriber and a box of scratched LP's are just a few of the potential friction points.

Changes to the house, even those that don't involve structural change, are always martially stressful. We have fought over pictures on walls, the appropriate usage of cupboards, the choice of bathroom tiles, the proper material for a kitchen worktop surface. Once, when the new sink taps were fitted without my knowledge I actually attacked the bathroom litter bin with a toilet brush in frustration.

So let no one imagine for a moment that this is a grown up, mature debate. As is no doubt obvious, when it comes to developing the house, I am an Eeyore while my wife is a Tigger. She looks for ways to move forward, I look for ways to stay where I am.

If it wasn't for her I suspect I would be living in a house that was more or less identical to the one we moved in 12 years ago. And perhaps this is a fairly typical male/female fault line. She is all Loft and I am all Basement – the woman always reaching higher, the man crouching in a confined space, looking for security in the damp and comforting dark.

AM I JUST A MAN WHO HAPPENS TO LIVE ON THE PREMISES?

How much should a man know about his family? I don't mean in a deep psychological sense, but in grasping the inconsequential minutiae of everyday life. Such a grasp, I have been made forcibly to understand, symbolises intimacy and caring.

Thus my wife is irritated when I can't tell her the name of the mother or the father of a particular child that one of my children go to school with. I will always make a desperate suggestion, using a popular forename that I have vaguely heard mentioned before - Adam? Jake? Melissa? - but I rarely guess correctly. There are just too many of them and they all look much the same.

Harder still is remembering the complicated names of the children who my wife sees most days at the school gates. Who the hell is Keshawn? Did Kumbaa really have a sleepover only yesterday? But this knowledge appears to be required of me. My wife seems to think that it means I simply can't be bothered to give all these people space in my overcrowded yet inappropriately airy head.

Knowledge is very far from being neutral in a family relationship – or more accurately, the retrieval of knowledge from the faulty ATM of my memory bank. It has often been said that knowledge is power, but it is also emblematic. How much of a father/husband am I, really? Or am I just a man who happens to live on the premises?

The fact that I do not remember than names of many of the teachers at the school my children attend is not forgiven despite the obvious justification that nowadays I can hardly remember the names of anyone outside my immediate family. No - It is a sure mark of that greatest of fatherly crimes, disengagement.

The truth is, I *am* disengaged. I am bound to be, because I leave the house every morning and do not return until the evening. Furthermore, I do not want to be engaged. I am not particularly drawn to other people's children

(with a few notable exceptions). I just like my own, and most of the time, I do remember their names (although obviously I get them mixed up now and then).

I often feel I am on some domestic version of University Challenge when my wife suggests to me that is absurd, even disrespectful, not to know the name of a street three blocks away when I have lived her for ten years. She has a perfect grasp of local geography, whereas I feel no need for this knowledge. After all, I have an I-phone with a map function. But it appears I am missing the point.

Most unforgiveable of all, I struggle with birthdays. I am fairly au fait with my own, and several of my children have easily memorable dates – Eva has hers on June 1, which is a doddle – but the others have weird dates that just don't stick in your head very easily. I mean, who can remember 18 September, which is definitely somebody's birthday. It's completely random.

Does this mean I am uncaring, uninvolved, disengaged? Possibly, but there is a very encouraging book I have just read called 'The Secret Life of the Grown Up Brain'. This confirms what I had hoped – that while your peripherals go to pieces after the age of about 40, and you spend your time walking into rooms then trying to understand why you are there – your core functions remain more effective than ever.

Perhaps my core function should be my family, my local topography and the night which Kumbaa or Keshawn had a sleepover.

And perhaps that's a choice. But then I wouldn't be able to write books any more, or chew gum and walk at the same. That's my story anyway, and I'm sticking to it. At least until I forget it and have to think up a different one.

HOW TO SUPPORT YOUR PARTNER

This is what I know about support. I know how to support a football team. I know how to support an argument with evidence. I know how to support a shelf with a bracket. What I'm less sure of is how to support my wife when she's going through a tough time.

It seems so easy when – say - I listen to 'The Archers'. The supporting characters say things like 'Don't worry, I'm sure it will be OK'. They make cups of tea and they sigh and they offer hugs and listen sympathetically, while the character in crisis responds gratefully. Real life crises are more complex.

Whenever I notice that my wife is in need of support – and I can't always tell - I find myself sliding into The Archers paradigm. It is inadequate. All I do is - at best - annoy my wife, and at worst infuriate her. I say the wrong thing. I do the wrong thing. More frequently still, I don't do the thing that I might have done, the thing my wife wants me to do – whatever it is, which I can rarely work out.

How can one do better? The problem is with support is partly one of a paucity of imagination. Sadness, depression, being under intense stress, going through a life change - these are intensely solitary experiences. What the sufferer really hopes for is to be known and understood while going through these traumas. But such crises of the soul are difficult to penetrate. It takes an unusual amount of not just sympathy, but empathy, to find the way through, to imagine your way into the same place.

I think both myself and my wife, when in crisis – she has to deal with my occasional but disabling depressions - tend to look towards friends as an alternative source of consolation. Women, particularly, often have strong support networks outside of coupledom.

A conversation with friends is baggage-free. When you seeking sympathy from your partner, it is easy to get caught in the trip wires you have set yourself in a relationship. If you say, 'I feel lonely and unsupported' it is easy for the other person to say, stiffly, 'well I'm doing my best!' to which the response must be 'It's not all about you!" And there lies the slippery slope.

Within a relationship, attempts at support can easily be couched in terms of the success and failure of a particular marital skill, and thus comes loaded with the expectation and the potential for praise and blame. This makes it tough going, for each attempt to ease the burden of the other becomes a sort of competition, or task.

This can be counter-productive. One resolution of this dynamic is to stop trying. I admit that when my attempts to console my wife are rebuffed – perhaps because of clumsiness on my part - I find it harder and harder to continue.

For what lies behind the bland phrase 'having a bit of a hard time' – often code for something much more serious - is the harder prospect of the failure of words or deeds to reach sadness, to heal it, to touch it. And thus within it lies less of an opportunity for intimacy than the potential for alienation. It is hard to help one another, when the pain lies beyond words or actions. One must keep trying. But it takes courage, imagination, determination and an unusual degree of emotional intelligence.

I wish I had more of any one of those qualities than I actually possess – so that I could learn to comfort others in the way the soap operas so deceitfully promise is natural and easy. For it is not a zero sum game. To console another is to console yourself. For that to happen the giver has to know how to give. However - and this is the forgotten part - the receiver also has to know how, and be willing to, receive.

A FUNNY THING HAPPENED TO ME

A funny thing happened on the way to me writing this column. Two funny things. Actually, come to think of it, one of them wasn't that funny.

Firstly, I took my youngest kids, Eva (10) and Louise (6) to see James Campbell's stand-up comedy for kids at London's South Bank Centre. Secondly, I accidentally read some 'jokes' tweeted about the victims of the hostages at the BP plant in Algeria by Frankie Boyle. (My sister-in-law's brother, incidentally, was one of the British victims. He was blown to bits. Boom boom, eh, Frankie?)

First, James Campbell. I was dubious that 'stand up for kids' made sense. Louise shared my concerns. 'Is there anyone else in the show?' she muttered, tersely, after ten minutes.

In fact, James was very funny, although possibly the adults and the older kids got more of the jokes than Eva. But I lost my doubts about how effective a specifically 'standup for kids' comedian could be.

Much of Campbell's comedy was, like adult comedy, purely observational. But it focused on things that were central to children's' lives - lollipop ladies, scooters, babies, hi-vis jackets on school trips, playtime - instead of, say, work and sex.

There were plenty of gags about old people. This, I suppose is about fear of decay and death – the 'laugh of relief'. Campbell got a lot of mileage out of the idea of a bath with a door in it for the elderly (these apparently really exist.) and the ridiculous shriveled wrinkliness of those two or three generations above the audience.

I am wary about analyzing humour too much. If I tried to work out why my own children find me so hilarious – the fact that I'm old, have a willy and a hairy bum, smell funny etc. – I might find myself discomfited by the fact that they are actually displaying the relief from primal fears about decay, sexuality and death, and the Elektra-complex desire to kill their father.

What struck me mostly, though, was the complete absence of malice in the laughs. This may because Campbell is squeamish, but it is more likely that up to a certain age, say 11 or 12, most children simply don't find malice funny. Otherwise, the fundamental impulses are the same as for the audience of Frankie Boyle – discovering incongruities, relieving ourselves of anxieties, recognition and surprise, and of course, the busting of taboos (there were a fair sprinkling of boob, nipple and bum jokes). But the whole affair is much gentler.

How do we go from chuckling at such innocent targets as granddad's wrinkles to victims of terrorist atrocities? When do we slip from banana skins to satire, from prat falls to poison? When children lose their innocence, perhaps it is never more on display than in the field of humour, where the pun and the willy joke can take second place to the sneer, the knowing snigger, the comedy of hate.

Frankie Boyle would not get far in the face of an underage audience – unless he showed them his bum. If he then shoved a cucumber up it, it would probably be doubly funny – at least to me. But jokes about the death of hostages would just be met with blank incomprehension by Louise and Eva, and probably tears.

Of course, children get a laugh out of *schadenfreude* too. But there is a qualitative difference between laughing at someone who has slipped on a banana skin and someone who has just been blown apart by an explosive device. Children know anyway. It's just a shame that some adults forget how to tell the difference.

But this is a column about children's humour, not Frankie Boyle's. So here's my favourite kids' joke version of the comedy of hate. Frankie, feel free to use it.

I hate Russian dolls.

(pause for effect)

They're so full of themselves.

Aythangyou.

A DEATH BED LETTER
TO MY CHILDREN

I am dying. Not imminently – just at the same rate as everyone else, but I think the concrete fact of the matter means that I would like to write a letter to my children before I go.

It is traditional to wait to do this sort of thing on your death-bed, but why wait? I can never get my four daughters to listen for me on such matters without sniggering or accusing me of pomposity. So I'm going to write it down instead.

Dear Jean, Rose, Eva and Louise,

It is not easy dying. But you'd better get used to it, because however young you are, it's happening to you, right now. So the first piece of advice I would give you is, don't waste any time.

This commonplace trope comes with a sting in the tail. Living by it, many people suffer a kind of low-level panic, a desperate rush to cram everything in before the final curtain falls, along with an inability to enjoy any of those things because they are snatching at them so desperately.

So – make an effort, but don't clutch at the world. Many things, good or bad, will come to you anyway, despite your efforts. The majority of life is luck. The more you chase after life, the more it eludes you.

This apparent paradox leads to my third piece of advice - cultivate a healthy attitude to time. The modern world has somehow contrived to expand the past and the future and shrink the present down to a tiny slice on the dial of a clock. Don't get hung up on what has happened or will happen. You can't control either. The present is all you've ever got.

All life is paradox. Nothing can ever be finally worked out. Everyone – scientists, priests, politicians, teachers, your parents - pretend they know what's going on. But nobody does. Life is a mystery. Don't run away from that mystery by cloistering yourself in some lie about the big importance of your job, or by losing yourself in some crazy cult or religion or compulsion. Embrace ignorance - not knowing is what makes life worth living. To know everything would be hell.

Love is the most important thing in the world, but it isn't as easy as an adult as it is as a child. Loving flows naturally towards you and from you now, but when you get older you understand the price, and the complications, of love. The biggest of these is that to love someone is to love also their flaws. This is made easier by never forgetting, that you, too, are made up of flaws. Mistakes, stupidity, error – they're all normal, everyday occurrences.

So - don't judge others, or yourself, too harshly. Try and be kind, but don't be so kind that people take advantage of you.. Don't forget that you can regret doing the right thing as well as doing the wrong thing. And don't let anyone ever tell you that right and wrong are purely relative. They are real, but they are hard to know.

Living is tricky, and everything is a guess. To see yourself through, what you need more than anything else is faith - faith in yourself as an entity that can survive anything the world throws at you. And you survive not by resisting the world, but swaying with it, by absorbing it. Be tough, but be flexible.

There's much more I could say, but attention spans are short, and don't fool yourself that people are listening because they are paying attention. So the last thing I want to say is that as a young man, my one certainty was that I never wanted children. Now, looking back, I know that in my whole life nothing has brought me as much joy as being the father of four. Which just goes to show how wrong I can be, and you will be too. And that's just fine.

Your Loving Father

THE FRAGILITY OF INNOCENCE

What is it that is most appealing about children? Is it simply their physical beauty? Is it their openness to loving and being loved? Their playfulness, their innate humour?

Beyond these things, in my view, children are beautiful because they possess something that we have all lost- the quality of innocence. Innocence is not merely lovely, it is heartbreaking, because it represents Housman's 'blue remember'd hills'...the 'happy highways where I went/and cannot come again'.

The gap between innocence and experience is endlessly explored, like a gap in a tooth, by artists and writers. I have felt in exile ever since childhood— not as a result of some traumatic experience, but the simple, slow dimmer switch of time passing and imagination coarsening.

But what is innocence? Like St Augustine on the subject of Time, 'If you do not ask me what time is , I know it; if you ask me, I do not know 'When I watch my youngest daughter, Louise, playing for an hour with Sylvanian families while singing to herself, I know I see it. When I watch my ten year old, Eva, dancing as if no one is watching I know I am also seeing it. But it is ineffable.

It is, at one level, a rarefied quality of ignorance. To not grasp imaginatively that death will come. To be ignorant of sex, likewise. To believe in the irrational - Santa Claus, fairies, monsters under the bed . And of course the myth of the infinite power and goodness of parents.

This is perhaps the hardest part of all innocence to let go of. My eldest, Jean, nowadays seems perpetually disappointed in me, and I can only ascribe this to the fact that I have let her down by proving unable to either be perfect or protect her against the world. After all she was forced to face the separation of her parents when she was only 6 years old. But I feel, self defensively perhaps, her disappointment is more about her particular loss of what we all must lose.

Innocence goes deeper than ignorance. It is some mysterious operation of the imagination, the part that can enter into mental universes from which one soon to be forever excluded. I have my own particular recollection of this.

Every year from when I was of reading age, I was given a Rupert the Bear annual for Christmas, and every Christmas day I fell upon it with a passion, losing myself deep in the mysterious tales of Chinese wizards and sea-gods and wood sprites. Then one year I picked up the annual and could not 'get into it'. It was just a book with pictures and a story. I could no longer enter its portal and inhabit its world.

Even now I remember the sting of disappointment. My wife thought I was mad when last year I bought a large painting of Rupert from the artist Mark Manning (who has done a series depicting scenes from Nutwood). But I suppose therein lies the explanation.

Innocence is also the growth of self-consciousness, perhaps the 'tree of the knowledge of good and evil' that is referred to the story of Adam and Eve. Perhaps you are thrown out into a world bled of colour and meaning and spent your life trying to regain it.

But can you regain it? Not in its original form, certainly. But sometimes, now I am growing older, I feel shadows of my ancient innocence in the night sky, in the song of birds, in the earth's breathing out of white and pink blossoms.

I am unlearning all the things I have been taught in life, and perhaps this, as well as the more tragic meaning , is what Shakespeare talked of when he wrote that the final age of man is . "Last scene of all, That ends this strange eventful history, Is second childishness and mere oblivion"

UNHAPPY BIRTHDAYS

When I used to go to birthday parties as a child – which wasn't often – I might take a card. I then would get sandwiches, crisps and lemonade and play a few party games.

Now, children's birthdays have expanded to epic proportions. Not only, it seems, does every child have to be invited to every other kids rarely make it through a weekend without some crayon-scrawled RSVP dropping out of their schoolbag - but said invitees each have to bring a) a card and b) a substantial gift for the special birthday bunny.

After any one of these beanos takes place – which nowadays may involve a visit to the cinema and/or restaurant/diner as well as a number of professional children's 'entertainers,' or a bouncy castle – the person holding the party is required to come up with a 'party bag' for each and every child who attends, which usually amounts to the same value as the gifts given by the attendees. Then there's the Thank You cards that act as a compulsory coda.

All in all, each and every birthday is an enormous MGM style production involving considerable expense and a great deal of effort – always, of course, on the part of the adults. The children just sit there getting fatter and greedier for pointless stuff and forced ritual.

The celebration industry is booming, leaking out of Christmas and birthdays into Valentine's Day, Mother's Day and Easter. It can only be a matter of time before I have to buy my children gifts to give me for Movember. I can only partly put this down to the extremely effective marketing campaigns of those who make their living from these sorts of occasions – card manufacturers, crap plastic toy makers etc.

Part of it to do with the sentimentality and indulgence of parents, but much more of it is about peer pressure. We do what we do simply because other people do it, and once the stakes are raised, as they always are, guilt forces us to keep up with the Joneses, lest our little darlings accuse us with 'but Wayne/ Scheherazade/Kemal/ Madison had a troupe of dancing giraffe clown acrobats at THEIR party'

I am often surprised that we are so often told our children are the unhappiest in the Western World – or something – which must be powerful evidence to the idea that materialism doesn't cut the mustard when it comes to a happy soul. However when I actually see the kids at these events, they seem to be having a nice time, though not obviously nicer than if they had just gone down the park together and climbed on the swings. It's the parents that are probably the unhappiest in the world, revolted by the greed on display, and checking their watch after ten minutes to see how long there is still to go before it all ends.

I am starting a Campaign for Real Childhood Celebration in which a) Birthday parties are limited to six attendees, none of which is required to bring a present and none of which will receive a party bag. B) All celebrations other than Christmas or birthdays will not require the exchange of gifts and cards. C) All parties are limited to 2 hours maximum D) All children over 6 must be involved in both preparing for said party and clearing up after it.

This is almost certainly an unachievable ideal, since we all crumble in the face of pressure from one another and within ourselves. I suspect children actually don't really care that much – give them a few sausages, a few simple games to play and put them in a room together with some paper hats and they'll happy. But the marketeers of happiness are too clever for us. It's not that they understand people so well. They simply understand guilt - and it makes them immense profits and us considerable fools.

PETS, SCHMETS

Our household at the moment is infested – sorry, blessed – with cats. Six of them. Having got rid of one, Dylan, last year – may he rest in peace, whining slob that he was - leaving only his infirm and senile brother, Floss, behind, my wife accepted a kitten. This kitten was promptly violated by the neighbourhood Toms and has just given birth to four of her own fluffballs.

I have to admit – the expression 'cute as a kitten' does not seem to be an arbitrary one. They are extraordinarily loveable. They mewl and simper and generally make the world a fluffier place. I like them. But I doubt that it will last. I am lifelong pet skeptic.

Confronted with a four-pronged Cute Attack it briefly slipped my mind why I was skeptical. I am now beginning to remember. The house is starting to smell of shit and wee. Worse than that, it reeks of that excremental cat food that you buy in sachets and anxiously squeeze out onto the plate lest it touch your fingers and contaminate you.

Cats come onto the bed in the morning at 6am, sit on your head and wake you up. They drink the water in your bedside glass. If you close the door, they wait outside complaining until you open it so they can sit on your head etc. Their lovability is more than offset by their extraordinary flair in the art of being annoying.

My prejudice is not confined to cats. To dogs I am positively averse. For start, they always introduce themselves by sniffing my groin, which I find both threatening and impolite. They are needy, time consuming, easy to trip over and they frequently smell bad. Also they have been known to bite people – certainly a lot of dogs in my neighbourhood appear to have specifically evolved for this purpose.

There are people – 'animal lovers' is the term, I think, collective noun 'posset' – who find people like me, people who care very little about other species, as barely human. If I were feeling apologetic about it, I would only say that I grew up in a house without pets, and therefore have never quite become acclimatized to them. My only pet was a stickleback fish that I caught in the canal and which died after six hours in my mother's household bucket. And a tortoise, whose shell I discovered to be mysteriously empty one day.

But I'm not feeling apologetic. Should I feel sorry because I can stare, awestruck by love at my children, but not feel the same way about another species? I cannot accept that people who don't much care for animals are emotionally defective. If anything, the reverse is true. The British give more money to animal charities than they do to children's charities. That is seriously messed up. Anybody who leaves their inheritance to a donkey sanctuary rather than research for, say, children's cancer research strikes me as profoundly cynical about the human race in general.

Human beings are difficult to love – they are complex, contrary and they often let you down. Animals, having barely a teaspoonful of brain matter, are simple and easy to love. But it's a soft option.

My children appear to adore animals, but in a highly partial way. They go all gooey about lambs frolicking in the fields and then sit down and eat their Sunday lunch with mint sauce but without a second thought. This is what is called sentimentality rather than genuine love.

But for the moment, cynic or not, I am content to have the gorgeous balls of fluff around the house. Three of them are being given away, we're keeping one, and Floss, by the look of his distended stomach and ratty fur – he's about 150 in human years– can't be for this earthly realm much longer. That will leave us with two. I can live with that, just about – so long as no one asks me, ever, to clean out the litter tray.

DOES GOD MAKE RADIATORS?

There are many disconcerting things about being a father, but perhaps the most unsettling of all is the recognition that there are a number of simple questions that you do not have the answer to. For the specialty of children is to ask simple questions, and these are the most penetrating of all.

At the trivial end of the scale, there are the philosophical inquiries one has to bat away about food and diet. Why, each of my four offspring have asked at some point, can't you have cake for breakfast?

It is pointless to point out that it is a matter of convention, because they will then suggest that the Almond Croissant I happen to be chewing on is, in fact, in nutritional terms, a cake, and that such a convention is routinely traduced.

The same might apply to Coco Pops, pancakes with maple syrup or even yoghurt and honey with crunchy granola. They are sugar, they are carbs. So why not a slice of chocolate cake, or an ice cream?

The only solution to such queries is to change the subject, ignore the question or shout. None of these responses are philosophically convincing to a child's mind, but they can make them shut up, which is at least something.

It has often been said, by me at least, that to expect a child to listen to reason is like expecting a lively game of backgammon with a hippopotamus. But the problem – as in the above examples – is not always the lack of reason in the child, but the lack of reason in the convention.

There are many other examples of such anomalies in every day life. If a child can't get to sleep until eight o clock, why make them lie in darkness for an hour, bored? Why not let them read until nine o clock and then fall asleep of their own free will? Because bedtime is eight o' clock, and they went to sleep when they wanted, well, chaos would rule. Wouldn't it?

Such debates about the efficacy of adult reasoning are not an occasional interruption in family life. The more or less constitute family life, with the added frustration that children have a licence to be irrational when they feel like it while adults are meant to act as scions of logic on par with Hegel or Nietzsche.

I asked my nine year old, Eva, about why she was so often mean to her younger sister, Louise. "Because she is my younger sister" she answered. "And that is what older sisters do to younger sisters". Her logic was impeccable. But I made her stop anyway. How? I threatened her. She cried. Now as a result, she can blame my corrupting influence for bullying tendencies. She wins every way.

Why do you have to dress your children nicely against their will, when they are happy to go out in horribly mismatched, creased and dirty clothing? Why do they have to have their hair brushed when you tell them they are beautiful anyway? Why can't they miss brushing their teeth for one night, since in the course of a lifetime it isn't going to make any difference? Why is OK to eat lamb for Sunday lunch when you've just been petting them at the zoo? Does God, as my 5 year old asked, make radiators?

I cannot answer any of these questions, but I do not want to do my children the disservice of letting the light in on that particular secret. I lie to them about the fact that I don't know what the hell is going on or the reasons for most of the things that happen in the world.

Why? Because that is one place that the relentless logic of the child does not want to penetrate. They'll understand that soon enough. And they'll come to understand the grim truth – that Mummy and Daddy were paper gods all along.

THE POVERTY OF EXPECTATION

Last week I found six-year old daughter, Louise, and myself yelling bitterly at one another as we walked down the street on the way to the tube station.

It wasn't like I was forcing her to eat broccoli. I just wanted to take her to the zoo. But she didn't want to go the zoo. She wanted to stay at home and do nothing.

This is so far from my experience as a child that I just can't get my head round it – which is why it made me so angry.

There is a gulf of mutual incomprehension here. It made me feel like when I've taken lot of time and trouble to make a good, delicious and interesting meal – rather than the pasta and baked potatoes I usually serve up – and be faced with a chorus of gagging noises and screaming fits.

Something weird has happened to childhood which has to with prosperity. Children are given good food they don't eat, taken on cool trips they kick against and are offered presents they never wanted in the first place. It's what you might call poverty of expectation, and I can't work out if it's good or bad, my fault or their fault or someone else's fault entirely.

This is particularly relevant at this time of year - obviously. All my Louise wants for Christmas is some Charlie and Lola books. Will she only get Charlie and Lola books? No, she'll get a huge bag of expensive crap that she'll get bored and irritable with minutes after receiving it. And then she'll get told off by her parents for being selfish.

Is this the child's fault – the consequence of their limitless greed and acquisitiveness? Or is it the desperation of the parents to give the children what they think they ought to be grateful for that is the problem?

That's where the morality of giving gets a bit murky. We all know the feeling when we wait for the face of person for whom you buy a gift to light up in joy and gratitude. That is your recompense for spending all the time and money spent tracking it down for them. 'Occasion' advertising always focuses on that expression of delighted gratitude. But it is very elusive, in reality – almost always with adults, but even children under-perform.

This pisses everyone off – because perhaps adults have become not the loving, generous people they envisage themselves to be, but gratitude junkies. 'You'll thank me when you're older'; comes the refrain when the child learning the violin complains. In our imagination of the future we see our offspring skipping and burbling with their appreciation of – us. We took you to the zoo, we bought you expensive presents, we taught you the violin. Now its payback time. Give us the smile, the flush of pleasure, the look of love.

The process of giving is vexed and complicated. How far are any of us from saying to a fractious child 'after all I've done for you' and them, inevitably responding, 'well I didn't ASK for it'? Perhaps our selflessness is not selfless at all, but a desperate attempt to assure all parties that we love our kids as much as the Jones's.

In reality, if everyone was by law limited to spending, say £50 on their children at Christmas, I doubt that in the long run any child under ten would really mind in the slightest – any more that any child would probably mind much if they sat around watching TV and eating junk food every day rather than being dragged out on endless day trips and being forced to eat polenta. Children demand very little beyond love, chips and protection.

Having said all that – we had a great day the zoo. That's the trouble with kids. They don't have a clue really what they want, still less what is good for them. In this they resemble nothing so much as their puzzled progenitors.

PERSECUTED BY THE FUN POLICE

The trouble with Christmas is that they generate a lot of Christmas parties, at which it is considered more or less compulsory to have fun. Trouble is, I don't really do fun anymore.

Fun, at 56, , is something of a spectator sport. Fun for me is watching my children have fun, or watching people on telly watch people have fun, like at the Olympic ceremony. But the capacity for fun itself, its essence, is rather like hair – it tend to fall away as the years pass.

I have been to a number of Christmas knees-ups with my wife. Lots of other people turn up with their wives and they all go through the middle-aged simulacrum of fun - what I call the funulacrum. They drink, they talk above the noise, and as the evening goes on, they flirt, they dance, and possibly even sing.

I slam dunk into bed about 11, slinking off early feeling a bit ashamed and hoping no one notices.

I have duly been designated a wet blanket. But the problem with adult fun is it seems to last so long. If you turn up at 8.30, you are seen as a lightweight if you go home before 1am. That's four and a half hours of fun. Isn't that a bit excessive? Even children's parties rarely last longer than two hours. And they don't have alcohol to slow up your metabolism and they don't go on beyond your bedtime.

I actually do really enjoy a few hours at a good party, just as I enjoy a few hours having dinner with friends. I love the food, the company, the, cough, 'vibe', as I believe it is known on the 'street'.

But I think the cult of the middle-aged party is a leftover from the young person's party, and as such is something of a conditioned reflex.

I understand what's in for anyone still young. For teenagers, staying up late is still a bit transgressive. Also , for anyone under the age of 40, there is a sexual charge to the evening, since young people are relatively attractive and available. The possibility of sex is what really fuels young adult fun, and that pretty much disappears by the time you're over the mid-life hill.

I admit, however, that I was never that good at fun even when I was in my 20's. I have always found a lot of noise oppressive, and the truncated nature of most party conversations frustrates me – I tend to find one person I hit it off with and stick with them most of the evening. Also I was always really crap at picking up girls.

But to be anything but brimming with enthusiasm for parties – in other words, being more introvert than extrovert – is laying oneself vulnerable to being accused of being a killjoy, even though you're not killing anyone's joy but your own.

My bookish 10 –year-old finds much of the same reaction when she takes a book with her to read in the playground. It's considered anti-social. But as Susan Cain points out in her excellent TED talk, 'The Power of Introversion', introverts are not unrealized extroverts – they are a separate species, with their own tolerances and tastes. No one criticizes a sociable person for not being solitary enough – why should the opposite apply?

Christmas is the season for extroverts, and I'm glad it's there. I genuinely do like a bit of wassail and revel. But when I've had enough, don't call me a party pooper. I don't want to poop anybody's party. I just happen to think that being by yourself can be better than being stuck a room swapping broken sentences with drunk people over loud music - even if the music is good and the people are loveable. And making yourself unconscious through sleep rather than drink is some of the best fun I know.

HOW TO HAVE AN ARGUMENT

The season of peace and goodwill is over. Time for a reality check. Let's talk domestic arguments.

I hate arguments. I always lose them, even if I win them, because I'm very thin skinned, so whatever the logical substance of the argument, and whether my point is good or not, I end up feeling bruised.

Arguments – unlike their distant cousins, discussions - are painful as well as inescapable. When you feel attacked, it is instinctual to fight. This is logical – if someone punches you, your animal self will hit back. Retribution should acts as both a defence and a deterrent. The trouble with this formula is that it doesn't work. You are simply raising the stakes. It's like trying to put out fire with petrol.

There are a lot of things I don't agree with Jesus about – I think we're going to have a long wait for the meek to inherit the earth – but his idea of turning the other cheek does have a lot of sense to it. The more you can absorb the blows; the more heat goes out of the argument.

But this is not a perfect solution either. What tends to happen is that if you don't respond you swallow the hurt and save up the bile for a future occasion. Also, passivity is not always experienced as passive. Once I went through a very Zen-like period in my life when I hardly ever responded to any goad. My wife found this very provoking.

The love didn't spread – it soured. In fact this is probably why they killed Jesus – not because he claimed to be king of the Jews but because constant forbearance is so fucking annoying.

There is also the matter of self-respect. Either partner in a marriage can only take so much hurt before they feel themselves humiliated. At those times, a show of anger seems to be demanded, if only to defend ones perceived sense of dignity.

There are people who can absorb hurt and disable it at the same time – those rare people who find strength through gentleness. Jesus was one of these people (although even he lost his temper occasionally).

I'm not very much like Christ. In fact I can think of few people I am less like. I fight to defend the vulnerable spot within when it comes under attack. I fire arrows through the slits in the turrets of my ego. And the burning boulders come right back over the battlements.

The way through this is tough and demanding. Instead of defending one's vulnerabilities, one has to own up to them. Instead of building walls, we have to raise the portcullis and lower the drawbridge.

This takes a lot of courage and trust. Sometimes I find that courage and trust, sometimes I do not. Often it depends on how much of those qualities I'm being shown in return. But someone has to start the ball rolling – not just once, but time and again, since one is bound to fail and fail again if one can ever hope to succeed.

I do have a rather naïve belief in love as being the answer to our destructive behaviours – something I also agree with Jesus about. But the word 'love' has so many meanings.

The philosopher Mark Vernon in his excellent new book 'Love' talks about Anteros – the brother of Eros and the god of conflict within love. Anteros, says Vernon, is a more realistic symbol of erotic love than the more sentimental Eros – because he represents the path by which one can build a genuinely authentic and mature love by negotiating the minefields of conflict, rather than the peaceful Elysian fields of romance.

Through negotiating our painful differences, we come to what truly bonds us together. Not a kind of pink jelly of icky sentimentality, but a tough construction born out of the twisted and broken metal forged when two people honestly struggle to recognise and respect each another's differences.

NEW YEAR'S RESOLUTION

I have decided, in the hope that it will help me to stick to them, to go public with my family New Year's resolutions for 2013.

*These pledges do not constitute a contract and may be varied at any time without notice. The value of these of these resolutions may go up or down.

Those resolutions in full:

I hereby resolve that I will never accidentally leave the keys in the front door again. This is a danger to the security of my family, who are quite liable to be murdered by one of any number of the psychopaths that roam the streets of Northwest London looking for just such an opportunity. The least that is likely to happen is that we will be robbed of all our valuables. Except that we don't have any valuables, but I resolve not to mention that, because it's not the point.

I hereby resolve, in fact, that I will never forget anything again, including the dates of birthdays, holidays, and Christmas, the night we're meant to be going to the theatre when I thought I was playing tennis and the fact that women, particularly wives, remain oppressed on a daily basis by the fucking patriarchy, which includes, by definition, me.

I hereby resolve that I will never again complain about getting my food last at mealtimes. I recognize that this does not indicate, as I seem to think, that I am the least important member of the family. I resolve to think that it is childish and archaic to think, even momentarily, otherwise. I accept this truth wholeheartedly and without reservation. I promise that I will be sorry that I ever thought it in the first place.

I hereby resolve that I will not watch TV or look unduly relaxed and happy when there is shit to do.

I hereby resolve that when my wife has three pillows out of the four in the bed, and she is asleep, and the only way I can get my pillow back is to risk waking her up by taking one of the pillows, I will sleep with one pillow, even though I can't get to sleep with one pillow.

I hereby resolve to never, ever lose my temper with my six year old again just because she WON'T DO ANYTHING SHE'S TOLD EVER WITHOUT SCREAMING HER HEAD OFF . Honest.

I hereby resolve to bake cakes like all the New Man-ny kind of chaps that my wife's friends apparently without exception married, cook more imaginative meals for the children which they won't eat, remember the names of all the pupils who are in their class in school and the names of all the parents of those pupils, and where they live, and generally behave like any good mother would.

I hereby resolve not to eat any of the children's sweets when I've got the munchies on.

I hereby resolve not to use my wife's toiletries which I ripped off from hotel rooms around the world when I'm doing travel writing. Not that I know where she hides them anyway.

I hereby resolve not to ask questions when a cheque from the joint account has been written out by wife which I don't know the reasons for. This indicates a lack of trust which is despicable and issues around money which probably stretch back to childhood trauma which is no excuse for my being a dick.

I hereby resolve to never, ever ask my wife for a taste of any of the food on her plate, while granting here the right, in perpetuity, to take anything from my plate.

I think that's it. Oh, and I hereby resolve never next year not to make any New Year's resolutions Because they are simply deferred factories of guilt and self-reproval and they never ever work.

In fact, I've decided not to put it off any longer, and make that my resolution this year instead.

NEW YEARS DAY: ON FRESH STARTS

It's the New Year. A fresh start suddenly seems possible. But is there any such thing?

Most of us have fantasies about starting again from scratch – particularly in our relationships. By the time you have been in a marriage for ten years or so, it's like a taxi cab that been working the streets of Bangkok – characterful, but beaten, battered, with scratched paint and windows that get stuck.

The fantasy of starting again is universal. The most potent words in the advertisers' lexicon are New! and Improved! . We talk of those New Year's favourites, 'purification' and 'detoxification' as if they could render our organs, bones and muscles newly generated.

But can relationships be renewed? Does even leaving them really give you a fresh start? No. There are no fresh starts – there are only inflections on patterns that were laid down long ago.

This does not mean that we cannot improve the relationship we are in. But it's a slow, incremental process, usually with a two steps forward, one step back pattern. People are complex, creatures of habit and reluctant to change.

The closest I ever get to a fresh start, strangely enough, is when someone close to me dies. Bereavement somehow cleans the windscreen of the soul, sieves out all the dreck, if only for a short time. You see straight. But the cold, glittering glass soon mists over again.

The trouble is, just as we take ourselves with us wherever we travel, we always take ourselves with ourselves into the future. A new partner, a new resolution does not change us. We are too deeply ingrained in too many ways.

This is not only true when we are old. I believe I'm at heart the same old slob I was when I was in my 20's. Dennis Potter always said that he spent his life waiting for a revelation that was just round the corner which never arrived. I have often had the same feeling.

I know, all the same, I am different to how I was 30 years ago – but I am, at some levels, exactly the same. And any changes I have been through have not come from resolutions or flexing of willpower, but through the hammering out of circumstance.

Which is why even having been through two marriages, I face the same complaints from my partners – and to some extent, have the same complaints against them.

Yet I am not despairing about this apparent intractability. People in relationships can amend, somewhat, long-established patterns of behavior, so long is there is goodwill on both sides. I also think we tend to give the past rather too much power in our definition of the future. After all, it is not the past the purely creates the present - the present also creates the past.

A real fresh start in a relationship would, in a sense, be to give up looking for fresh starts – to stop looking back over your shoulder at the past, which needs to be escaped from, and the future, which you are anxious to arrive at .

In reality, there is only now and this present moment, and it's a question of negotiating that moment – if negotiating is the right word. Perhaps live the moment is better.

This is, of course, a Buddhist point of view (not that I am a Buddhist). Buddhists also say all authentic action is unmediated and spontaneous. This is where a fresh start lies – with the realization that the past and the future are entirely artificial, not with goals and targets and the straining of sinews and tendons of your so-called will.

This does not mean you can't change things – it just means that you can't change things by endlessly pontificating on how you're going to change things. The fresh start is inside. The only change you can really make is to realize that.

TECHNOLOGY ATE MY FAMILY

I once wrote an article called 'technology ate my marriage'. It recorded how, since the introduction of the Internet, mobile phone and PC, my wife and I spent less and less time in face to face contact, even when under the same roof.

Since then things have got worse . Technology is eating my entire family – myself included. Virtual space aces physical space every time. Rarely can any single individual be found in the house at any one time without earplugs stuffed in the side of their head and their digits dancing over a touchscreen.

I pleaded for my ten-year old daughter not to be bought a Kindle Fire for Christmas, knowing full well what the outcome would be. It was to no avail. She has spent at least 20 per cent of her available time since December 25 completely out of Earth contact. Her principal family is now The Sims.

My wife and I can no long simply sit and watch a film on TV together. She is tweeting simultaneously, and spends more time with her eye s on the computer s than the TV. It's not what I would call a shared experience. Likewise – until I insisted she stopped – she would take her computer to bed and surf while I was trying to slumber in the flickering light of her pixels.

My eldest daughter has been known to text me from another room in order to ask for a cup of tea. Meanwhile, though we have had long had a ban on watching TV during schooldays, I now find my six-year-old watching re-runs of My Little Pony on You Tube (computers are allowed, see). And this is all before either of them have a mobile phone.

I would like to claim that I was the virtuous exception to this virtualization of family life, but I have been gradually crumbling into the habits of everyone else. Now I access my computer first thing to check my tweets and read the Guardian. I suffer what my teenagers call 'tweet incontinence', pinging off inappropriate messages to the wider world about what should be purely domestic affairs., thus stoking conflict. In the evenings I can often be found playing online scrabble with a friend whereas I used to play real scrabble with my real wife.

I am going down with the ship into the whirlpool of electronic half-life. This all has a positive side. The web has made the world more interesting. Too interesting. Real life, real people, real members of the family are dull and problematic in comparison.

But the real richness that is to be found on computers, tablets and mobile phones is too often overtaken by the slough of habit. The same people who would sneer at others for keeping their TV on at all times happily sink their lives into cyber-world, perhaps under the illusion that it is inherently more intelligent, and 'human', since it is interactive.

This is open to question. Telly-junkies have given way to cyber-junkies, and I am not sure that an hour in front of 'Angry Birds' or on some dimwitted Twitter feed is any more nourishing to the soul than, say, an hour in front of some halfway decent TV programme. And yet it is socially acceptable. I think the same kind of controls should be put on technological devices that *bien-pensant* families used to put on TV watching.

I have become aware lately that when you institute talk with a stranger, they look extraordinary startled, as if you had broken some fundamental taboo. I suspect that people are becoming programmed, at family level, not to deal with genuine flesh and blood humans.

Which is why we need to put away the gadgets – at least for a while. Actual life may be duller, and more prone to conflict., than virtual life. But it has this one, signal advantage. It is real.

FOOD FASCISM

Of the many battlegrounds on which one fights in a family, food is one of the most poisonous – which is ironic, since it's meant to be all about nutrition.

There are many fronts to this war, but the most fundamental is getting your children to eat what you want them to eat rather than what they want to eat. This is most poignantly represented in literature in Jonathan Franzen's 'The Corrections' when the one of main characters tries to teach his son to eat his food, leaves him at the table until he eats it, and then accidentally forgets about him and goes to bed leaving him stubbornly stranded till the small hours.

The idea of forcing their child to finish their broccoli, or beans, or whatever green object it happens to be, is one that most parents try sooner or later. That's how they find out that it doesn't work. Nothing, in fact, works. And the more you bully your child into eating the 'right' food, it's my personal view that the more likely you are to end up with a teenager with food issues. They are likely to come to associate eating with stress.

I am not saying one should leave children to sustain themselves on crisps and chocolate bars. I'm merely pointing out that the need to make our children 'eat well' may be rooted in matters other than the well being of the child. In my early years as a father, the issue of getting my children to eat what I wanted them to eat was an issue that drove me to fury. I remember one epic battle that I tried to get

Jean, then about 8, to eat a single pea. I failed. And I was furious. But I doubt that it was really fury about the fact she wasn't getting enough vitamins.

Louise, my youngest daughter, is similar in her determination to limit her diet to whatever she likes the taste of. This doesn't vex me so much any more, partly because I have become lax and fatalistic about parenting, but also because I believe she will grow out of it. Also, nutrition is a very inexact science – I understand there are tribal cultures in which a very narrow range of foods is consumed, and yet produce healthy, well-nourished adults. Nevertheless I still get mightily irritated if I, or my wife, have gone to the trouble to make a 'proper meal' – something involving other than rice, potatoes or pasta – and she responds with a pointed 'yeuch!'.

If only the frontier of the battlefield ended there. But my wife's reaction to my cooking is much the same as Louise's to hers. Much more able at the stove than me, she tends to be dismissive of my efforts. I tried doing a barbecue recently, and after several complaints about the correct temperature of the charcoal, I tetchily handed the whole thing over to her. When I try to prepare anything, she has a tendency to stand over me to make sure I'm doing it 'right' – i.e. her way.

When I first met her, I hadn't really done much cooking, and served her up something from a 1970s cookbook involving tinned sardines, raisins, pine nuts and pasta. She has never forgotten this, and has since decided that I am some sort of debased, archaic version of the Galloping Gourmet (one of the first TV chefs, with an affinity for prawn cocktails and gammon steak). I cannot seem to escape this pigeonhole for all my Diana Henry/Nigel Slater inspired efforts.

For food isn't simply, or even primarily, about nutrition or even enjoyment. It's also about memory, control, love and much besides. And it's not only anorectics and bulimics who have an unhealthy attitude to it. It's rather like money, in that we all project our own personal obsessions onto the subject. Because when we feed one

another, we are not only serving up portions of food - but great dol-
lops of meaning.

TO FORGIVE, DIVINE

A friend of mine recently ended a 25-year marriage. When I asked him why, he said, 'too much past'.

It struck me as a sad, but illuminating, phrase which contradicts the mythology of marriage - that time brings a deepening and an enriching of a couple's lives together. We share memories, experiences – childbirth, tragedy, marriage itself – that create a common ground that both wife and husband walk upon.

Yet factual memories are, after all, phantoms, moments that have gone forever and only remain as pale reflections. Some people remember the good times, some remember the bad, but as superficial snapshots of times gone they lack power.

The past that lives in the present is the emotional, not the objective past – the world of feelings, rather than facts. The reality of pain and conflict tend to endure because they more often than not are rooted in issues that remain unresolved.

In a long relationship every new moment of disharmony or disagreement can feed into a previous version of exactly the same argument. I sometimes think that couples only have seven or eight rows. They are the same arguments repeated again and again, and their force only increases as the years pass, because the frustration increases each time they flare up again without being solved.

Thus the mantra becomes 'you ALWAYS do this' or 'you NEVER change' or 'Why can't you EVER listen'. The past builds up to act as a negative force on the present, eventually having the power to dissolve that present entirely.

How can one come to terms with the past? After all, a past is inescapable - the moment after you enter into a relationship, there it is. The first and the hardest thing is to be honest. Most unresolved arguments remain unresolved because one or both of the people involved are not being truthful. For to be honest means to confront, really face, the problem, and it often seems a lesser price to pay than to keep playing out the same drama over and over again, even it is a constant sore.

But honesty alone doesn't solve anything. It is just a step towards something more important - the capacity for forgiveness. Everyone is capable of selfishness, of stupidity, of not acting with the proper respect towards the other partner in the relationship. Yet we usually cast ourselves in our personal dramas as pillars of virtue, with our partners, in our minds, the supporting characters who always come up short.

This renders forgiveness very hard to achieve – and even if it is achieved it has a patina of self-righteousness that renders it unwholesome. For real forgiveness, I think one has to acknowledge the log in one's own eye before one can forgive the splinter in another's. It's pride that makes forgiveness hard.

Even if pride is swallowed, forgiveness is only a possibility. The actual mechanism of forgiveness is mysterious. What one finds nearly impossible to forgive, another finds a matter of simplicity. And thus another layer of mutual misunderstanding arises.

It is simplest to forgive someone when they acknowledge their fault. But given the machinations of pride, they rarely do – especially if it is a deep fault. So one key to a relationship is forgiveness even when none is asked for – perhaps even when the behavior that is requiring forgiveness still persists.

This is a tall order, and one that carries no guarantees of success. Forgiveness may well go unrecognized, and all the efforts that might be made to achieve it. Thus it can add another transgression to the list of crimes to be forgiven.

Yet in the end, lacking forgiveness is punishing yourself more than anyone else. Hate and anger and resentment lodge in the heart like cankers. However, for the past to become liberated from all its barbs and tripwires, this is the only way to go – away from the past, into the present, towards the future.

WHY DEATH MATTERS

It's been a difficult week. My 87-year-old father has been in hospital and his prognosis isn't good. An extended family member has died, suddenly and brutally.

At such times, the profound importance of family is reasserted, underscored, brought into relief. My daughters singing Happy Birthday to me over the phone as a shuttle back and forth to my father's bed. The kind concern of my wife and all my friends.

One discovers the hidden truth about life in our cynical world, the secret my father always insists on - the profound amount of goodness in the world. The endless offers of help, the waves of goodwill and concern.

I am reminded of the messages hanging in the air, after 9-11, the finals codas to lives inscribed in digital code, hanging in that perfect blue sky, finding their final expression on mobile phones, on answering machines, on tinny speakers. *I love you. I love you. I love you.* This is the deepest of human impulses – not postmodern disconnection, but its everyday opposite, authentic, untarnishable.

I am not afraid for my father, or myself or for any of us. When the darkness comes, as it must, one can only stand in front the shadow and understand that it the other side of the light. You cannot have heads without tails.

Can I hide my tears from my children? From my father? Should I? I try to. Yet I believe in truth, and that one can't protect even children entirely from the facts of the world. To deceive them is to exclude them from a crucial, inescapable part of life, that of loss and of change.

My father always believed in taking life on a day-to-day basis, and that philosophy is serving all of us well. To see a man so big, so physically shrunken is hard. And yet he is still him – the chuckle and the smile still intact in the face of whatever is coming to him, emanating from grey skin, vocal chords that struggle to manufacture words to attach to his thoughts and feelings.

One is also brought hard up against the reason for the apparent indifference of the wider world to pain and suffering. Compassion hurts. It means, 'suffering with'. To care about someone, to love someone, is to hurt for them as well as for yourself. Easier in some cases to cut yourself off.

What are we to do with death? How are we to face it? Neither I nor my father believes in an afterlife. But I do believe in death being necessary – that a world without death would be unbearable.

Death brings everything into focus. It purifies and clarifies. It is awful, yes, but not so awful as we make it, in our denial of temporality and change and impermanence. The impulse to cling on is very human, but it, not death itself, is at the heart of human tragedy. Life is dissolving smoke. To cling on to it is like clutching running water with your open fingers.

I know very well that these sentiments can seem glib. The hard part is still ahead, and there is sadness, of course. But there is also the recalibration of the inner self, not just for me, but for all our family. It isn't that someone is dying that causes the worst part of grief. It is the part of them that is in you dying that is the hardest part. The process we call letting go.

I will -inevitably - write about this again. In the meantime, a line from the great drama, 'Six Feet Under' runs again and again through my mind, when a grieving relative asks Nate Fisher, the funeral director, the question that all of us want an answer to, and he somehow answers truthfully, hopefully, without being brutal.

"Why" she asks, imploringly, "does there has to be death?"
"Because" he answers, "it makes life important".

JESUS HATES YOU

"Jesus loves you" my 5 year old, Louise, remarked the other day. 'That's nice', I murmured. Eva, Louise's 10-year-old sister, had a more pungent response. "But Jesus hates *you,* Louise". Exit devout child in biblical flood of tears - perhaps to pray for divine retribution.

This is the latest chapter in a series of theological debates that have taken place in our household. All my four daughters have attended church schools and the younger two are regular churchgoers. Only the five year old seems to retain any semblance of true faith and it appears to be under existential threat from her older sister.

These questions of God and Jesus are ubiquitous. We went to see the Lion and Witch and the Wardrobe in Kensington Gardens – the Christ story dressed up as children's fiction. Jesus Christ superstar is about to open at the O2. Eva and Louise's grandfather has just died, and they watched their granddad Dingle, via a light oak box, being consigned to the arms of the Lord.

Religion, for parents, has its uses. The idea of consoling your children by telling them that when you die you go to heaven, however, has a limited shelf life. They usually start to doubt before the age of 10. I recall my eldest, then 9 years old, talking jauntily about death, and then pausing, her face clouding with horror. 'But what if there's *nothing* after you die?" She burst into bitter tears. I was silent. I couldn't bring myself to utter the story about heaven one more time.

I have deeply mixed feelings about Christianity. I am glad my children go to church and even glad that they go to a church school. I don't know why. Perhaps its because these institutions are primarily middle class and I am a snob. Perhaps it's because a part of me believes that some sense of morality is genuinely instilled in children, although my eldest were educated at primary level at a non- religious school and don't seem any the less moral for it.

But at a certain stage religious faith has to be put aside, if only to be re-embraced later. I would be concerned if Louise reached her mid teens and still believed that Jesus loved her, or me, or anyone else. If she hadn't reached a stage of healthy skepticism by then, I would assume she was vaguely maladjusted.

This is not to disparage all the good, worthy and quietly decent Christians. But I think that if the faith isn't seasoned first through a life of hard knocks and genuine testing – as Jesus was tested - it does represent a form of brainwashing. There's something wrong with someone who won't question their childhood beliefs. My two older children have now adopted the default British attitude – they don't believe in anything in particular, and muddle through the best they can without any particular consistency or sense of reference to an external source of morality, outside peer group or family.

The meaning of the Christian story to me is not a moral tablet of stone, but as a mythic story, with a central core of truth that is rewritten in different forms over and again. This is the idea of renewal through sacrifice which is a template that finds its way into countless pre and post-Biblical narratives.

This is the lesson I would like my children to infer from the medium of religion – that life is all about the repeated death of self, marking each new stage of life, and renewal of self only comes through that death. This has been my experience of life and will be theirs. It is universal.

This is at the heart of the Crucifixion, understood through an adult eye, that only through the willful embracing of the pain of negation does the soul – and the world - transform. And whether you're watching 'The Lion King', or 'ET' or reading 'Beauty and the Beast' or 'The Last Battle', that message endures, buried but ineradicable.

CHILDHOOD ROTS THE BRAIN

Much has been written about the effect on the development of the personality by parents on their children. Relatively little has been published on the developmental influences of children on parents.

Personally, I am convinced that neglect by a child towards an adult can lead to long terms damage and a negative effect on ones cognitive and social ability. I recently went to a fairy-based event at the Globe Theatre in which my 9- year-old daughter and I were invited to search Bankside for followers of Oberon and Titania. On that dismal shore, I had an epiphany: enough fairies already.

For the last eighteen years, I have had to deal with the shifting terms and conditions of the tooth fairy (including the current sterling – enamel exchange rate) and catalogue the various genii of flower fairies. I have innumerable Rainbow Magic Fairy Books (just try reading a few sentences without wishing to scoop your brains out and stamp the produce into the compost heap.)

Fairies are just the beginning. The dumbing down of this particular adult through girly kiddie culture probably started with 'Where are You Blue Kangaroo?' which I have now probably read around 50 times. It's a nice little book – but I haven't read '1984' more than twice, and that's got a lot more interpretive potential.

When I start thinking about the long hours I have spent marshaling Sylvanian families into various makeshift residencies, or watching 'In The Night Garden' or much worse, 'My Little Pony', or trying to understand Moshi Monsters vernacular (worse than

Geordie) - I think it is surprising that I have any working mental equipment at all.

Standing around in playgrounds for hours pushing swings, often two at the same time, can be soul destroying, but it is not actively abusive in the way watching the hideously miscast movie version of the Magic Roundabout.

The above activities merely make me stupider. But then there are the many activities that produce long-term emotional damage. My daughters, for instance, like to play noughts and crosses on the criss-cross wrinkles on my forehead. If that's not abuse, I don't know what is. And they never get pulled up on it, do they? Why? Being cute isn't a defence in law, after all.

Who knows what trauma I suffered trying to get each of my daughters in turn to learn how to ride a bicycle. For god's sake, IT'S NOT THAT DIFFICULT. Just don't BLOODY FALL OFF. A BOY WOULDN'T FALL OFF. But of course, I can't say that. I have to be nice, don't I? And get them a present when they finally, eventually, after god knows how many tries, tears, and complaints, actually do something that any adult knows is VERY EASY.

No, I'm damaged all right. And it's all their fault. God, that time I spent half an hour trying to get one of them to eat a pea. One single pea. I offered her the world, and still she wouldn't eat it. I still can't read 'Eat Your Peas' by Kes Gray and Nick Sharratt, which bravely addresses this very issue, without twitching and having flashbacks.

I suppose there have been occasions when I have been culturally and psychologically enriched by fatherhood. Certainly, I am happy to treat 'Hippos Go Berserk' by Sandra Boynton as valid adult bedtime reading now. The quality marque is also awarded to 'Horrible Histories', 'Wonderpets' and 'Rugrats'. But on the whole that is putting a stalk of broccoli up against an entire MacDonald's menu.

But perhaps there's a biological sense to it all. Certainly the consumption of Girl Kiddie Culture for all these years has reduced my brain to mush. And if I have to hear the theme tune of 'Peppa Pig' once again, I may indeed run down the street brandishing a cleaver. But then again, I am supremely well adjusted to the challenges of senility. And for that, I suppose, sooner or later most parents will be able to thank their children.

COMMUNICATION BREAKDOWN

I have written before about marital communication, mainly from the angle of my wife and I often choosing to avoid it, since we find it so painful. But sometimes we actually find a way to kick down the walls and make it happen.

We have a number of 'loaded' topics in our relationship - ones that are so contentious that they invariably lead to heated argument. The most difficult things to talk about are almost always the most important ones, the ones that are quietly eating away at your marriage behind a wall of silence.

One of the most effective techniques to find a way through this barbed wire fence is an exercise I call 'Silent Witness', which we learned on a 'marriage course' my wife and I took last year. And yes it was, cough, part of the Alpha Course - you know, the one for, cough, Christians - but actually it was pretty smart, and inexpensive and you could do worse than try it even if you do worship pagan idols.

This is how it works. You make an agreement that one of you talks, while the other is required to stay silent, making eye contact, but banned from responding *in any way* – either in words, sounds, contemptuous snorts, or body language.

The listener, having heard the speaker, then 'reflects back', and sums up what he or she *thinks* the speaker has been trying to say. The speaker will then either confirm or correct the listener's impression. Then the listener asks, 'what the most important part of what you've just said'. Finally the listener asks 'and what do you think we can do about it?'. The speaker responds, the listener remaining silent. *Fin.* Now it's the listener's turn to speak.

Artificial as it sounds, it's very effective in forcing one another to listen. And once you've actually been properly listened to, the heat tends to seep out of the situation, without the other person having to say a thing, or offer a solution, or commit even to some kind of change.

Another aspect of communication breakdown lies in the different emotional languages people speak – also pointed up in the marriage course. For instance, I like to hear my partner say nice things to me, as often as possible. You know, "I love you" and other vaguely encouraging remarks. She rarely does, however.

This – I learned - is not out of indifference, but out of the fact that she experiences the demonstration of love in a different way. Words mean little to her, deeds everything. If I want to show my love for her, looking at her like a mooncalf and uttering the words "I love you" doesn't cut the mustard. Cutting the grass cuts the mustard. That's love expressed as deeds. My wife's showing of her love for me, in her mind, lies in her doing the washing, taking on the bulk of the childcare, making me supper, not in 'sweet nothings', which in her mind are exactly that – nothing.

So now if I want to show my wife that I love her, I hang up the washing or hoover the carpet. It's altogether more effective. Sometimes she even tells me that she appreciates it – which comes no more naturally to her than unblocking toilets does to me. But I love to hear the words, which to me mean more than deeds.

To learn one another's language sometimes feels harder than learning Mandarin Chinese - simply because you have to step into someone else's shoes and other people's footwear is usually uncomfortable.

But without understanding the meaning of deeds as well as words – and the meaning of words as well as deeds - then any relationship is liable to flounder, not on intrinsic difference, but simple misunderstanding.

Because although communication is natural to humans, good communication is as rare as hen's teeth. And the difference can be, starkly, the difference between the survival of a marriage and it's extinction.

WHY GET MARRIED

At the weekend I was walking on Hampstead Heath with my wife. We were both trying to remember why we got married.

This was not so controversial a conversation as you might imagine. It wasn't a 'why the hell did I marry YOU' conversation. It was more a gentle puzzlement about why we felt the need to buy into a certain social institution that at some level, neither of us are – so to speak – wedded to.

After all – we reflected – getting married had made no difference to our relationship. It had not made us any more or less secure, or any more or less happy. It had been a wonderful day, but we were exactly the same people with exactly the same relationship, and the same joys, problems and difficulties afterwards.

My wife is a feminist, and one happy to describe herself as such. For any feminist, surely, the nuptial state is one that is rooted in patriarchy, ownership, and exploitation. Why would any independent minded woman want to go there?

For myself, twice married, I found myself doubly puzzled. I had never esteemed the Christian institution of marriage, and yet, despite being an atheist, I had married in a church on both occasions.

After my first marriage broke up, you might have thought I would have been disinclined to go through the process again. It wasn't the marriage I objected to so much, but the divorce, which, apart from the personal bitterness, cost me half of all my wordly goods.

So I was wary of marrying again – as much as anything else for purely practical reasons. Stepping outside the pink cloud of romance, the hard facts were that more second marriages broke up than first marriages. Perhaps I was setting myself up for another fall that could see me end my days living in a bedsit and beating at my brains with my fists like Lear to drive out the folly therein.

But there was an inconvenient fact at the heart of all this emotional calculus. I wanted to get married again - albeit mainly because I thought it would make my partner happy, and I wanted her to be happy. After five years together, I finally asked her. She said yes. And then she said no.

Why? Because she asked me, hard on the proposal, the killer question, "are you asking me to marry you because you want to, or because you think *I* want to?" Busted . She withdrew her consent. Which in one stroke got me off the hook – and yet simultaneously removed the reason why I might think I would be on any hook in the first place. She clearly wasn't after me for my money.

The subject was thus shelved, until a few years later when we had two daughters. Four of us were walking in Regents Park, on the dead days on the far side of Christmas - my two daughters by my first marriage and my two youngest. This time it was my partner who asked me. And I said yes, without thinking about it.

'Without thinking about it' is perhaps the crux of the matter. The Buddhists say that the only right action is unmotivated – that it is not a matter of deciding on the basis of whether something is 'good' or 'bad' but choosing on some deep instinctual level. And that is what I did.

As, last week, now married five years and together for 12, we reflected on why we got married, my wife came up with the simply, compelling answer which had nothing to do with security, convention, money, religion for commitment.

"I married for love" she said. And so did I., and could only ever marry for love. For marriage is lovely for its very superfluity. No more explanation can be asked for or made.

WHY CHILDREN'S TV ROCKS

I recently wrote a column stating that I believed my brain had been rotted by eighteen years of being exposed to kiddie culture – Barbie Dolls, puppet shows, shit movies with talking animals etc. But as with so many of my opinions it has recently occurred to me that I was entirely wrong.

I have misremembered all the cultural gems I would have missed out on if I had never had children. And actually, I think I've had more pleasure out of kiddie culture, most particularly books and films, than I have out of reading all manner of literary novels and art house movies.

The main scapegoat for the deleterious effects of kiddie culture is usually held to be American Kids TV programmes. This is what is fingered by parents as brain rot, contrasted with our supposedly more wholesome homegrown produce.

But when people think of American cartoons, they still tend to think of low-grade poor quality conveyor belt material that the adults of today grew up with – Mutant Ninja Turtles or Transformers for instance. But now the summer holidays are here and TV is a necessary prop to see you through, I am reminded, daily, of how startlingly good American children's programming is.

I had the good fortune to have my first child in 1993, which was right at the beginning of an unacknowledged golden period of American children's TV –unacknowledged because most TV critics, then as now, saw children's TV as peripheral to the supposedly more intelligent adult TV.

In these golden days of the early 1990s, ground breaking new series such as 'Aaaah! Real Monsters', 'Rugrats' 'Ren and Stimpy' and the 'Animaniacs' changed the game for American cartoons. In contrast with their 80's predecessors – the awful 'Scooby Doo' (still incomprehensibly remembered fondly) the Smurfs and Alvin and The Chipmunks these programmes were ironic, multi layered and dark

'Ren and Stimpy' cartoons were frequently censored for being too violent and deranged. 'Animaniacs', an updating of the old Warner Brothers cartoons (the main characters, Wacko and Jacko were meant to be the original Warner Brothers, along with their lesser known sister, Dot) threw in so many cross-cultural references as such a speed it was hard to keep up in between laughing. 'Rugrats' was a dry American sitcom set amongst children, and 'Aaagh Real Monsters', a precursor of 'Monsters Inc.' film was just plain weird – and genuinely creepy.

I spent countless hours glued to the TV in those days (computers for the children were not yet an option) and I never had so much fun. It all went of a bit belly up towards the end of the decade, when the 'Powerpuff Girls', 'Pokemon' and various low grade Japanese Anime cartoons began to crowd the airwaves, but by the time my two youngest were born, in 2003 and 2006, the Americans were back with a vengeance – most notably with the awesome 'SpongeBob Squarepants', 'Futurama', and 'Phineas and Furb' (surely best performance ever from a cartoon platypus). Weirdest of all was the operatic, 'Wonderpets' about a hamster, a terrapin and a duck who saved pets in peril in a flying boat while communicating entirely in sung verse.

The first time I saw 'Wonderpets' I thought it was deranged crap. The next time, I realized it was genius. Certainly the libretto from 'Wee Wee Pee Tinkle' about a puppy who is stuck in a house when needs to relieve himself is up there, for my money, with Wagner's 'Tristan und Isolde'. 'Dogs do it/Fwogs do it/Even muddy oinking hogs do it/Sooner or later every one has to go/wee wee/pee pee/tinkle'.

All this revolution was kicked, of course, by the genius of the Simpsons in 1989, which to this day remains the favourite cartoon of all my four children. Yes, nowadays the Brits have got Horrible Histories, Charlie and Lola and much else to be proud of. But don't diss the Yanks. Childhood – and parenthood – would be immensely impoverished without them.

I MISSED MY CHILDREN.
THEY KEPT MOVING

I have been away from home travelling for most of the last four weeks. I've enjoyed it – but I have missed my family each and every day. It is like a wound that won't heal until I walk back in through my front door.

Only the first part of the first sentence of that paragraph is true. The fact that I imagine 95 per cent of people would have actually believed the last part is evidence of what a state of denial we are in about the concept of 'missing' people when we go away.

We are hooked into the verbal convention of 'missing'. 'Missing you already' we say as we walk out the door. 'Missed you SO much' we say, when we come back. Isn't it at odds with how we actually feel? It's rather like asking 'how are you' - a figure of speech, an arrangement of words disconnected from meaning.

Missing someone has nothing to do with how much you love them. I would fight a full-grown baby crocodile to protect my children, and a slightly smaller and less dangerous animal to defend my wife (this has been proven – I once trapped small, angry frog under a bucket when it invaded our hotel room without flinching much). I miss my children fleetingly, even intensely, but it passes like a memory.

Missing an adult more than slightly, to me, betrays a measure of insecurity. I am connected into a web that is family, and this web supports me when I leave. No single nexus of the family unit is permanently necessary. It is the connections that matter, the matrix that supports all individuals.

I only miss two categories of people – the dead, and those who have abandoned me, i.e. those who have left the web, or who disappeared before they could become part of it.

My two younger children - reportedly - really do miss me when I go away, and sometimes acutely, to the extent of shedding tears. I am touched by this, but they also miss their teddy when it gets concealed under a cushion. Also, children are not adults. They really do need those around them. Adults should outgrow this. We are all semi-disposable.

My wife never says, 'missed you darling' when I come back from one of my extended visits abroad. Faintly disappointing though that is, I take that as the mark of a healthy relationship. It means my wife is a complete and independent person. Thus I can travel without guilt.

The truth is, the waters close over all of us swiftly when we go away. Why should it be otherwise? Is my personality so thrilling? Is my tagliatelle with Gruyere, pine nuts and tapenade so delicious that the family will fall into ruins in its absence? I am made of the same dull mud of humanity as everyone else.

I rather suspect this semi-detachment may be more of a fatherly than a motherly impulse. Mothers, when they go away, worry that standards will drop. Lunchboxes will be packed with candyfloss, Monster Munch and chewing gum. Bad American cartoons will be watched wall-to-wall. Slobbery will break out like a virus.

Mothers sometimes fail to understand that although this is often true, it does no one any long-term harm. The painful truth is, they are dispensable – at least temporarily. And I suspect what mothers miss is not their children or spouse, but the opportunity to keep both under their protective gaze.

Love and need are very different matters. I love my family and I need them, but I do not need them all the time. You cannot love anything that lives with the shadow of need, because all things change., and all thus all things disappear. Children stop being children. The wife you married is not the wife she is now, and neither are you the same husband. All is in flux. Only the web is constant, and it supports us all.

WOMEN ARE BETTER
THAN MEN – OFFICIAL

Having had the privilege of four daughters and more than one marriage, I have spent a good deal of time trying to underpin my self esteem against a persistent creeping subsidence of female disappointment in my gender makeup (once known as 'masculinity'.)

I have always fought my corner, suggesting that we are not actually somewhat defective versions of women, but a fully realized gender on our own part, with our own special skills and talents and propensities.

However, the evidence against this viewpoint is mounting. A survey last month suggested that women are now scoring higher in intelligence tests than men. For the previous hundred years, men scored about 5 points higher, but that's all over now. We are officially the thicker sex.

Women are now conspicuously smart in areas where they were once told they were stupid. Men, meanwhile, are on a historic quest to discover their limitations and women have been very willing to help out. Which is nice.

Once, for instance, men didn't know that they were emotionally inadequate. They believed that being distant and separated out from their emotions was their role as fathers and husbands. Women have redefined this as a deficit rather than a virtue, and men have taken them at their word.

The shortfall applies not only in the matter of emotional and intellectual IQ. My daughter, Eva, mentioned the other day that she "preferred girls to boys because girls have a better sense of humour, they are less violent and prettier". It's hard to disagree.

I used to stand against this consensus of male shortfall, seeing it as a sort of cultural cringe. However, I'm running out of road. I have observed enough marriages, including my own, to accept that men, in most cases, occupy very much the supporting role to the prime mover, the wife/mother.

We still do 'better' in the world of work, statistically speaking. This may be to do with sexism and that old, spectral enemy The Patriarchy, but I feel it is also partly because women, especially mothers, are often intensely conflicted about competing at the same joy-destroying level of intensity in the career world as men.

It's true that men continue run the political, military and financial establishments, but perhaps this has to do with men *wanting* it so desperately. These areas are the last bastion of male values - raw aggression and risk taking. As such they are not much to be proud of. Men's only real clear area of superiority, in brute physical strength, has become irrelevant.

Last year statistics showed that women aged 22-29 earned more, not less than men. Never married childless women actually earn more than the average man in the 30-something age group. Women's buying power dominates the economy. The most successful group of athletes at the Olympic was American women – and we are never far behind the Yanks in social trends.

Men, it seems, are simply not suited for the modern world so well as women.

There are still things I – shamefacedly - prefer about men to women. Like Martin Amis once admitted, my taste in fiction is largely homosexual. I prefer to watch men play sport than women – women's tennis and football for instance has never quite captured my imagination (although athletics is an exception.)

But on the whole in the bigger game, the game of being, women have come out ahead – maybe not yet in terms of power and status, but on terms of ability, resourcefulness and moral standing. This is good news for all my daughters, and it will certainly come as no surprise to my wife.

How do I feel about this? Not particularly delighted. But I feel I have taken a big step in admitting it finally to myself. Perhaps I am a modern man at last. How does it feel? Pretty much like women used to feel about male dominance, I imagine. Not that great - but impossible to gainsay.

ON THE DEATH OF A FATHER

The call came on a Sunday afternoon. My 87-year-old father, who was in a hospital on the Welsh borders, was suffering kidney failure. I had to get there fast.

I set off on the four-hour drive immediately. The weather worsened to a buffeting, vicious swirl. The snow was a million white scrawls etched on the night. Fog and mist and rain and sleet joined the chorus of weather.

I reached the small cottage hospital after the dark had enfolded everything. I entered the ward where my father lay. He was parchment and bone, but still handsome, noble, even.

I leaned over him. His eyes were open, cornflowers frosted with death. My tears fell, and ran down his cheek, leaving a glistening channel. He recognized me, and broadcast a smile that blistered like desert sunlight. He could hardly speak anymore. But even the clearing of his throat was specific and familiar, recognizably *him*. I told him I loved him. An answering rasp emerged from the depths. I understood the broken words completely. I smiled back in acknowledgement.

It took more than two more days before the end came. That time passed differently from how I had expected. Sad, but also tender and positive and beautiful. Death is so intimate —more intimate than first love. I could hold his hand, gaze into his eyes, stare unhindered at his tender face, stroke his frosty hair.

He was very thin, skin the colour of a dried corn husk. His mouth a dark tunnel. The jagged mountain ranges of his ruined teeth. The petrified forests of his hair. The failing locomotive of his breath. The sadness of the black, bobbled socks on his calves. Yet he was irreducibly who he had always been.

Much of the time he seemed unaware of what was happening. Then the veil lifted and he saw us and the sun shone through the pores and creases of his face. Such a smile. He would raise his eyebrows quizzically, as he always did, as if to say

'isn't this absurd'?

My brother arrived, then my eldest daughter. We grabbed sleep where we could. His wife, my stepmother, who adored him, slept on the floor by his bed. There was laughter, reminiscence, an unexpected joy.

My father's wife was appearing in a pantomime that week, as the villainess, all dressed in green silk with a feather headdress. She sashayed into his room on the last afternoon in full costume. Wonderfully, unexpectedly, my father laughed. I never admired her so much as that moment.

It was 3.15 in the morning when the call from the hospital came. I had finally retired to a hotel around the corner. I went to join my stepmother. She stared at me when I arrived, but she didn't see me. I tried to tell her of her bravery.

We gathered up our belongings, and left him his blue tracksuit to be dressed in for the last journey. He always loved that tracksuit. I gave my father a last kiss.

The next day the snow had come again. We went to the small churchyard, visible from the window of his modest house . Everything was cold and beautiful. His widow – how odd that word sounds - pointed out where she would like his plot. Where he could be seen from his home.

I wept – we all wept – but not for his life. He was fulfilled. He had spent his working life, happily, as a greengrocer. He was a good man, adored, almost revered, by his wife and family. He accepted himself. Not least of all, he loved his country and wanted to be nowhere else. He was fully content with his life.

The funeral will be soon. Black is to be prohibited. The daffodils will be rising, and my father will be distributed there, through the earth and the trees and the air. I will miss him, but I will never mourn him. His death, was, like the man himself, was profoundly average yet utterly exceptional.

BATTALIONS OF SORROW

Sorrows come, wrote Shakespeare, not as single spies but in battalions. And so it proves. The day after my father died, I returned to London, after weeks of emotional pull and tug, ready to spend a quiet night out with my wife. We took a taxi to the theatre. Halfway there, my wife received a hysterical phone call.

It was hard to hear what Eva was saying she was crying so much. Six-year-old Louise had fallen and hurt herself badly. Only Eva and Rose, still only 17, were there to look after her. We turned the cab around and headed back.

When we got into the house the first thing I noticed was the amount of blood on the floor. Rose and Louise were still crying. Our neighbor, who had rushed over, was sitting with Louise on her lap holding a blood soaked tissue to her head. Louise, rather than crying, looked frighteningly drowsy.

Our neighbor revealed what was underneath. Something inside me kept frozen, providing a buffer against the shock. A jagged rip in her forehead, flowing with blood, through which I could see bone.

The wait for the ambulance was spent trying to keep Louise awake and to calm Rose and Eva. The story emerged through sobs – they had been racing along the hall corridor and Louise had slipped and banged her head on the hall step.

My wife, an intensive care nurse for many years, knew that such severe blows to the head can lead to permanent brain injury, and the fact that Louise was so sleepy was not a good sign. We were both frightened, and determined not to show it.

The ambulance arrived after 25 minutes, the driver blaming cutbacks for the delay, at which point I felt the welcome distraction of a bolt of visceral hatred of the government. My wife set off with Louise to the hospital while I stayed to look after the other girls. If the death of their grandfather had been bad, this was worse.

Once again, for the second time in 48 hours, I saw the world I knew and had trusted to safely persist, dissolve. My imagination could not stop wheeling. And yet a part of me stood apart and watched the events unfold, almost neutrally.

It was several hours later that we heard that a CAT scan had revealed that her brain was undamaged. But she had to be taken to a different hospital for immediate surgery on the jagged rip in her head.

We all travelled to the hospital the next day to see her put under general anesthetic. Seeing your child put into an operating theatre was a trauma in itself.

The operation was successful. Now she has an inch and a half L-shaped scar on her forehead which, we were told, will fade in time. But that night will not fade in time. It was the night when natural loss was supplanted by the prospect of unnatural, unsupportable loss.

It is a wonder any of our children grow up. Jean nearly accidentally hanged herself on a venetian blind cord when she was four. A few years ago I fell down the stairs with Eva in my arms and cracked her head on the floor. Rose at 10 ran at full speed into a plate glass window. My niece Grace had to be talked round from the wrong side of a tenth floor balcony when she was three. My brother Jack was skimmed by a speeding car on a pedestrian crossing when he was a teenager.

Disaster is only ever the tiniest step away, and yet we must behave as it wasn't. Most children survive their childhood. But there is a moment in nearly every life when it might have so easily been damaged or taken away. It is always shocking, but afterwards the shock is erased, always, by piercing, desperate gratitude for things being just exactly as they are.

ATTICUS VS. HOMER

I took my ten-year old, Eva, to see the Regent's Park production of 'To Kill a Mockingbird' last week. Afterwards, I asked her, half jokingly, that if she saw me very much in the mould of Atticus Finch. She replied that she thought I was more after the style of Homer Simpson.

'To Kill A Mockingbird' is a book that has many themes – racism, innocence, the nature of justice. But what chimed most powerfully, and poignantly, with me was the portrayal of fatherhood – poignantly because the role model of Atticus, as a dignified, kind, worthy man who represents an ideal for the community and his children, has more or less disappeared from popular culture.

The most moving moment for me in the play was when, after conducting a brilliant but doomed defence of the unjustly accused black worker Tom Robinson, Atticus walks past the public gallery where his children, Scout and Jem have been watching. One of Robinson's supporters, Rev. Sykes, says to them, "stand up, your father's passing". They stand – proudly.

I found this very moving, because it is a model of fatherhood lost to the modern world. We are all Homer Simpson now. This is inevitable and justified for the culture. Centuries of women being second class citizens were bound, in the righteous backlash that is feminism, to curtail the status of men, who were revealed to be, rather than heroic, sexist, emotionally narrow and sometimes violent (like the 'bad' father in TKAM, the wicked and abusive Bob Ewell).

At a cultural level, no one could argue with the Simpsonisation of fathers, and the dominant portrayal of them in advertisements, popular drama and films as little better than children when they are not being violent or weak. Fathers, and men in general, had it coming. But I just wonder – isn't there a danger that the baby was thrown out with the bathwater?

For whatever is happening at a cultural level, at an individual level there are any number of fathers who are decent, dignified, kind and wise. I have even met some of them. Their role model – the person they aspire to be, whether they have read TKAM or not – is Atticus Finch, not Homer Simpson. But it that is now an unattainable idea, because the culture would stand against the acknowledgement of such a man, if he existed. It would be resisted with the same kind of force, although with different motives, as a woman who claimed she existed only to please men.

This is not merely a shame. It works against the interests of the very forces that seek to hold the dignity of fathers as questionable (as a compensation for the fact, at a mass level, that men continue to hold the political and economic levers). For without a good role model, adults react much the same as children – they live down to expectations. They will not make the effort if they know their efforts are doomed before they start.

Mothers, girls and women are not short of positive role models, but fathers, boys and men exist within a culture that holds them, at a purely personal and domestic level, second-rate citizens. Well, so be it – we are not so feeble, I hope, that we cannot accommodate this. But it must be especially hard, I think, for boys growing up today, particularly those with fatherless families – something in the order of 1 million in this country according to a report by the Centre for Social Justice this week - to think well of themselves and their futures with a default cultural position holding that they are always on the brink of backsliding into sexism, violence or simple incompetence. Boys need role models like Atticus Finch, and girls need fathers they can respect as well as lovingly mock.

'Stand up – your father is walking past' is an echo from a lost time and a time that will never return. But the echo itself must never be lost, or all of us, men, women and children alike, will be the poorer for it.

THE GREATEST TABOO

This week I am going to write about the biggest taboo in relationships I know. Not sex, not death, not bodily functions. I'm going to write about money.

Money in marriage is incendiary. It involves issues of power, feminism, patriarchy, trust and much besides. I have tried to write this column once before and had it flatly vetoed by my wife because she felt the ground I was treading on was too sensitive.

This column appears only after an emotional and sometimes painful back-and-forth about the subject. She accused me of sexism, while I suggested she was using double standards (I asked her, in her imagination, to switch the gender roles to see how it would look then.)

My wife works as a part time associate lecturer, and like many part time workers, who are predominantly women, tends to be discriminated against in terms of financial reward and employment opportunities. I, on the other hand, am reasonably well paid for challenging but not backbreaking work.

My wife does more of the childcare, cleaning and cooking than me. This is predominantly for practical reasons. She is physically at home for a lot more of the time than I am and, with a part time career, she has more hours available. She also tackles all the laundry, having rejected my offers of participation in that area after I shrunk a cashmere sweater, pegged it out incorrectly and turned a dazzling white load grey.

I have somewhat more disposable income than my wife – because I earn significantly more than her. Although I cover a good deal of the family, holiday and household expenses, she doesn't feel this gap in resources is fair. But I am not quite sure what might make a better alternative. The idea that when you get married all your finances merge into one strikes both of us as rather archaic. We both want to have our own money and bank accounts, rather than everything being in just one joint account.

The income inequalities also mean that if there's a big expense, like a foreign holiday or house improvements, I tend to have the last say. She feels that infantilises her, since she needs to 'ask me'. But we both recognize that in any circumstances where consensus is required- like large expenditures - we need to ask each other anyway.

My wife says that my having more money than her makes me feel powerful. She's right – up to a point. It gives me an area of control, although I don't think I use it in order to control. I just think some form of imbalance is inevitable.

When it comes to the house and children, my wife enjoys virtually total authority. She believes she has earned that authority by putting the most effort into it. The power gravitates to her and she feels more comfortable with that arrangement.

Likewise, I believe there is bound to be a certain discrepancy over the amount of authority in financial matters so long as I generate most of the finance. That is not to say I call all the shots or use the money to control my wife. I don't. There is just a discrepancy, and some measure of inequality in all marital arrangements is unavoidable.

We get by. I would say we have relatively few arguments about money. But it's tricky. There is a lot of counseling out there for emotional and familial difficulties in a relationship, whereas so far as I am aware, there is very little practical advice on how to run family finances. And yet a number of studies identify disputes about money as causing more arguments in a relationship than any other issue.

Personally I think the main solution is generosity of spirit and faith in the other person. I may be falling short in both these departments – in which case it isn't only the bank account that needs a top up. It's my trust fund.

MY CHILDHOOD VS. THEIRS

My six year old, Louise, asked me "what was it like when you were a child, daddy, in the olden days?"

I told her that my childhood was rubbish and that she didn't know she was born.

She picked languidly at her imported American Froot Loops complaining mildly that the milk was too cold.

Then she said, "But daddy, last year the Guardian ran a story claiming British children now were 'the most miserable in the industrialized world'.

"Really?" I said, nonplussed.

"Yes" she said. "And the Daily Mail agrees. They ran a story that said" "Children of Broken Britain among least happy in Europe"

"Oh, I said" I always thought you had it pretty good".

"Apparently not" she responded. "It seems things were much better in the 1950's and 1960s when you were growing up. It's one of the few things the liberal press and the right wing Tory leaning newspapers agree with"

I thought I might point out a few aspects of difference between my childhood and hers. But she turned away, abandoning her unsatisfactory cereal, and started playing with her Nintendogs console. So I thought I would complete the discussion here.

My childhood compared with my children's:

1. Holidays. They were crap. Cold and wet. In England, in Bed and Breakfasts that kicked out you after breakfast. My children have so far been to more exotic locations than David Attenborough. Yes, they're middle class. But you can get a package holiday abroad now for the price of pint and a packet of pork scratchings.

2. Boredom. My children are never bored. They have TV, IPods, mobile phones, PC's, games consoles, TV on demand, child friendly, free museums and exhibitions. Yes they're middle class. But even those on very modest incomes can afford basic versions of most modern technology.

3. Sleepovers. When did they happen? I never once had a slee-pover as a kid.

4. Getting hit. Like most kids, I would have to take a slap now and then. My children don't get hit. It's relatively rare nowadays. Yes, my children are middle class. You think its only middle class parents that don't hit their kids?

5. I was always peripheral to my parents' universe. I had to fit in with what they did. Sitting in the pub car park with a packet of crisps was as good as it got. My children are at the centre of family life. Yes, they're middle class. But I think it would be patronizing to suggest that it's different for the working class. And there have always been a minority of dysfunctional families.

6. Happiness. The Guardian report claimed that one in 11 youngsters (9%) aged between eight and 15 have a 'low well-being' at any given time. That means 10 out of 11 don't have low wellbeing.

7. Children in Britain report higher levels of satisfaction with school than almost any other European country.

8. Football. When I went to a football much I had to listen to racist abuse and unbelievably foul language roared by frightening men. And that was just the footballers. Also the soccer itself was of an unbelievably low standard. Or maybe that was just QPR.

9. Food was terrible. Boiled – all of it. What I would have given to have some good junk food – a MacDonald's or a KFC. But that was 'eating out'. We never ate out. I went to my first restaurant on my 18th birthday.

10. TV. It was crap. Now it's good.

I could go on. Yes, many childhoods are blighted by poverty, family breakup, and alcoholism blah de blah. But that was true 40 years ago, too (people got divorced less, but I'm not sure that helped anyone).

So that's what life was like in the 'old days', Louise. It sucked. Now – can I fetch you some more cereal? And this time I'll heat the milk properly. Sorry.

COMPETITIVE DAD

My nine-year-old daughter, Eva, beat me at chess this week. I didn't let her win. But she out thought me. No luck was involved, or mercy.

She beat me fair and square and she knew it. That's why I am reluctant to give my children quarter at games. Or perhaps that's a rationalisation. Perhaps I am more like the Fast Show's 'Competitive Dad' who takes games far more seriously than he probably should. Whether it's a five year old taking me on at snap or racing my teenagers in a swimming pool (they both can beat me now), I give it my best shot.

It is tempting to characterise this as disordered behaviour. I give into the temptation sometimes myself. If so, I can only do what my children are already learning to do – blame my parents. Both my mother and father were determined to win, even when I was at primary school. My father used to take my pocket money off me at pontoon and cribbage, without a twinge of remorse. He thought it was important to learn to lose, and delivered me a crash course in that discipline very early in life.

My father's philosophy was that to try your hardest, even against children, was to be honest to them, and show them the respect of a competitor to another. Even if you were foreordained to lose, because of your youth, you knew that when you did win, the victory was authentic. The symbolic nature of the activity is thus not debased by the condescension of parental pity.

In my all male childhood, (two brothers, no sisters), winning and losing was a big issue. My father was impossible to beat at tennis, because he would not give me the tiniest inch. However, when I reached the age of 17, I finally took a set off him after he had puffed and shuffled around the court with all the energy and determination that is 47-year-old self could muster.

It made me feel lousy with pity, but like most of my feelings it was mixed. There was pride there too. And this is the rationale – admittedly unfashionable – of not patronising your kids by letting them win at everything, just because they have smaller brains and limbs and look cute.

There may be a gender aspect to this. Although my wife is at least as competitive as me, and my eldest daughter even more so, there can often be an effacement of competition amongst girls. I have watched netball games in which the opposing team, instead of sulking and jeering, stand and clap when their opponents score a goal. This kind of admirable behaviour makes no sense to me, and I think it is essentially female.

I have done my best as I have grown older to damp down my competitive streak, with limited success. I've been known to throw the odd game of snakes and ladders, and show insouciance towards losing minor games of luck – Happy Families, Ludo – that I would have been incapable of 20 years ago. I still want to destroy my wife at Scrabble of course, but that is, I think, healthy and natural.

As far as children are concerned, I aspire to teach them that triumph and disaster are, to paraphrase Kipling, imposters, to be treated both the same. However, I am afraid that the words of that still greater philosopher, Snoopy the Beagle, are etched more deeply still on my heart "It doesn't matter if you win or lose. Until you lose".

I know that for a fact. Because when I lost to Eva at chess, I felt very proud. I hope she felt the same, because when she won she knew that no one was treating her as anything but an equal. And that makes her what I know she is – an authentic winner.

THE DIRTY BUSINESS
OF A SCHOOL PLACE

This is the biggest month in the calendar for anyone whose child is finishing primary school. The envelopes have dropped, the emails have arrived. The destination secondary school is set in stone.

In the end Eva got into a school that has ten applications to every place (#humblebrag) so we imagine it must be good, or at least, popular. But it's difficult to get to and looks like extremely hard work – they start at 8.30 in the morning, sometimes earlier, and don't finish till five. Plus there's a lot of homework.

As a bit of a loafer myself, that level of industry strikes me as intimidating. On the other hand, it's got a sibling policy, so I don't have to worry about where Louise is going when she leaves primary in four years. And it's secular, and co-educational, and state funded.

Most of my friends and neighbours seem to have got their kids into a school that they are happy with too, which is faintly annoying. I always feel much better about a choice when other people are disappointed in theirs.

An ugly sentiment, I know, but the struggle for a school is full of ugly sentiments. Competitiveness is never greater. The permutations are endless and the battles are bitter. After a struggle with myself, my elder children went to an all girls' faith school, and I prefer co-education and secularism. But they prospered, so I can have no regrets. This time, it is my wife who has done most of the struggling to find a school for our daughters. She put an immense amount of time and effort into it and it has paid off (although it is actually our daughters' achievement, not ours).

We are, I suppose, those 'sharp shouldered' middle class parents who think they can nag and badger their way into a decent school. Such parents are frequently derided, but I have never been quite able to work out why it is something to be ashamed of. Anyway, is there something to stop working class parents nagging and badgering? Don't tell me they're too tired/don't have enough time/are the victims of cultural inheritance. Everyone is free to make an effort for their child.

Are those parents who can't be arsed better than those who try to control outcomes neurotically? I suppose at least the not-arsed brigade is innocent of the sin of hypocrisy. After all, those who claim passionate support for state schools often cave when they end up in the local sink and send their child to the private sector (I put my first child into private school for a couple of terms, and I am still shamefaced about it).

Atheists embrace faith schools. Determined proponents of co-education send their kids to single sex schools. Vociferous advocates of multiculturalism hustle their kids into schools full of white middle class children. Passionate supporters of localism bus their kids to somewhere five miles away. Parents are brought face to face with the gap between who they think they are and who they actually are, and it can be very painful.

I dare say it's all in vain anyway. I dare say Eva, and my other children would probably have been fine whichever school they went to. They have the social capital, after all, but their parents lack the self-confidence to let the chips fall where they may.

I like to focus on an article I read a few years back, about a middle class family who sent one daughter to a posh private school and one to the dodgy local comp. Both children had trials to overcome - one the size and anonymity, the other the pressure of work and the

TIM LOTT

resulting distress – but both came out fine and both did very well, taking with them different worlds of experience.

As my dad used to say, it will all come out in the wash. Of which I'm glad, because getting a school for your child still feels like a terribly dirty business.

THE COMPENSATIONS OF OESTROGEN

It was the eighteenth of September 2006 when I realised I'd finally been converted.

My wife, Rachael, and I were both crying with joy and relief at the birth of our healthy new baby. Then Rachael said she was sorry. I couldn't work out what she meant. 'I'm sorry it's not a boy", she said.

I laughed. "I don't care." I was actually very happy it was another girl. Esme would be my fourth, along with Ruby (16) Cissy, (14) and the most aptly named of all, Lydia (7). Aptly because I, a writer of fiction, was gradually coming to resemble a fictional character – Mr Bennett in Pride and Prejudice (who numbers among his four daughters one Lydia Bennett).

My resemblance to Mr Bennett is growing. I am different from him in one way – two of my children are from a previous marriage. And Rachael couldn't be less like Mrs Bennett. But his world-weary amusement at the endless machinations, shenanigans, mysteries and subtleties of the female world have become deeply familiar.

I came into this oestrogen soaked condition entirely unprepared. I grew up with two brothers. My teenage and early adult years did very little to lift the mystique with which I had endowed women. They were incomprehensible creatures, who I thought to be vaguely morally superior as well being clever in a very different way from the way that men were clever.

Anyone who has been married twice – or even once - will know that the first of these propositions is, to put it mildly, dubious. And when you've got four female children as well, you learn too much to hang on to the idea that women are morally superior. They are with I might most generously describe as 'differently endowed' with morality. But they *are* clever in a very different way from men. Unfortunately, their cleverness is so different, I still haven't been able to work out how it works. But then again, I'm a man.

Before I go any further I should emphasis that I love being surrounded by women. This is partly because I am a very girly man. I like shopping for clothes, I like talking about emotions and relationships rather than football, I enjoy cooking and I even get a kick out of Celebrity Big Brother.

However, it isn't always easy – for them. In a recent photo session which involved taking a picture of all five of us together, the photographer made the memorable request of my wife 'could you just unclench your fist for a moment.' Perhaps its one another they find difficult. But, more likely, they have to deal with a father/husband has all the bluntness of emotional intelligence and memory that makes men, well, men.

Naturally I forget birthdays, school assemblies, Christmases and so forth. All men do. But my blindness goes deeper. I remember once blithely announcing, for instance, to my oldest daughter, eight years ago, that Rachael was pregnant (with Lydia) fully expecting her to hug her stepmother and burst into tears of joy. Instead, she ran down the street and hid. Rachael, needless to say, had confidently predicted such a reaction.

Females understand each other. They are also tremendously loyal to one another. Sometimes when Ruby teases Cissy I have tried to intervene on her behalf by remonstrating with – all, right then, shouting at - Ruby, But then Cissy turns on me and defends her sister like a tiger. It's incomprehensible. Cissy gets her relief by teasing Lydia, and Lydia hers by teasing Esme. I don't know what Esme does, but I fear for the cats, who have been looking very nervous since she became ambulatory.

But perhaps the most surprising thing about girls to me, brought up as I was around boys, is that they are *all different*. Every time I try to characterise them as a group in some particular way, I find an exception. Kindness, compassion, ruthlessness, selfishness, egotism, cruelty, generosity, helpfulness, competitiveness – all are distributed between each daughter in very distinct and disparate ways. There is no such thing as a 'typical girl' any more than there is such a thing as a 'typical' woman.

But they do have a few things in common that do distinguish them from males. They are highly territorial. They cry more than males do, and for different reasons. They are loyal to one another *as a gender* (which is why, that when things go wrong I make a handy scapegoat).

But the wonderful things about girls is that they don't hide their love. Boys start off cuddly enough, but usually end up aloof, playing their life game of being tough. But for girls, part of their life game *is* the expression of love. Thus even now the physical love between myself and my daughters is a daily form of balm and refreshment – the hugs, cuddles and kisses all co exist with the recreational mockery of manhood that women and girls nowadays both favour as their default form of communication.

I must stop now before the small remaining male part of me becomes nauseous. For I realise now what living in a house full of women has done to me. It has made me soppy. I drip with the candyfloss of pinky, sticky sentiment As a result, nobody is afraid of me, and no one listens to me much. It's a big blow to the male ego.

I try to reclaim my manhood sometimes, sometimes by retreating to a men-only Turkish baths, at other times an all male writer's retreat. But within hours I am missing the candyfloss. At times like that I know I will never truly be a man again. It's gone too far. I'm submerged in pink.

But you know what – in the end, I'd rather be hugged than slapped on the back. And I don't even mind that one no-one listens to me. After sixteen years surrounded by women and girls, I long ago stopped believing I had anything important to say anyway.

GETTING OLD

There are many markers for the realization that the thing you feared all your life – that you really *are* getting old – is finally coming to be.

Only last week, I found myself reading, *with interest,* the leaflets at the doctors entitled "'Are you finding your stairs a struggle'? and 'Do you sometimes feel shaky and dizzy?".

But the reality didn't really come home to me until I picked up my youngest daughter from nursery, and the carer asked her if 'granddad' was coming to pick her up in the evening.

I'm only 56. But there is no easier way for a middle aged man feel like an ancient than a) to have young children and b) have a younger spouse - my wife is 11 years younger than me.

Youth and age to a certain extent go together. It is often said, for instance, that grandparents get on better with children then parents. On the other hand, a young family acts as constant harbinger of decrepitude.

If I can't hear what someone says properly, it is immediately assumed by everybody that I am 'going deaf'. If I can't understand something that someone is saying I am, apparently, 'senile'. If I forget something, I am plainly in the grip of Alzheimer's (my wife actually insisted I go to the doctors for a test).

Growing older is never easy, but the idea that children- and a younger wife – keep you young is questionable. To be stereotyped in the family story as Dickens' 'aged P', nodding and mumbling in the corner, is to face the fact that families are more like lion prides than support networks. The old roarer, once he can no longer cut the mustard in the jungle, is pretty much slung out onto the veldt – although in the case of human beings, metaphorically rather than literally.

My wife often says that she would find living with someone of my advanced years much easier if I would 'admit' that I was going senile, deaf, potty etc. Yes it would be much easier, because then everyone in the family could agree that I had served my purpose and could be put into a home at the first possible opportunity.

Interestingly, when the real effects of my age come to the surface – for instance, I have a low tolerance of noise and chaos, and I usually take a nap in the afternoon – my age is no longer to be taken into account. I am, rather, considered boring and lazy.

But on the whole, I like growing old. My view of life feels more Olympian. Most of my main battles have been fought – only illness and death left, really, to face. I find it easier to live in the now, and I am no longer struggling for money and status.

Having a younger wife definitely has its advantages. I still fancy mine, for instance, although I'm sure the sight of me in my pants is unlikely to find her seething with reciprocal lust. Also the joy of children does keep one's proceeding crustiness at bay.

But I watch some of my friends who started earlier on the family project retiring, children having left home, free to start life anew, and sometimes I do have a pang of envy. Old age offers a new chance of freedom, but for me, that will come very late in life. Too late, probably.

Because by then, my family's presentiments will probably have come true, and I'll be dribbling somewhere in a bath chair by the seaside, my grown up daughters bringing be sympathetic grapes which I will misidentify as table tennis balls or kumquats.

Then they'll be finally able to say, triumphantly, 'we told you were getting old'. But fortunately, by then, I won't b able to understand them. And even if I can, I'm damn well going to pretend that I cant.

WHY MY DAUGHTER
WANTS TO BE SMACKED

I have often wondered – or perhaps a better word is 'fantasised' – about what is the best way to punish a child.

Once, it was simple. When I first became a father, nearly 20 years ago, an occasional light slap on the bum was not the taboo it is now. I only recall using this method on a couple of occasions, chiefly to stop my children running into the road without looking. It was effective.

I became very quickly convinced that whether it worked or not, it had to be abandoned on purely moral grounds. It seemed to me the same argument applied that led me to oppose capital punishment - it might act as a deterrent, but it was simply wrong and must be shunned.

However, I have felt the resulting vacuum of power since. Once you take away the smack, what remains? I asked this question of a child psychiatrist once, and he assured me that there was no need to punish children at all. The thing was, to reward them when they did the right thing, rather than penalize them when they did the wrong thing. This, he insisted, was much more effective than any negative sanction. This view has become a sort of received wisdom.

Doubtless in some world of research-led academia this is true. It is even true, to some extent in real life. We have all tried the star charts to encourage good behavior and it can achieve positive results.

However, this pat-on-the-back culture has its dangers. Whenever I have tried it on any of my four daughters, the strategy has quickly got out of control. Before long, I was being asked for sweets and money, simply to get them to say thank you for their dinner or pick up a discarded crisp packet.

So what else can we do to control children's behavior? (And they do need controlling. I'll take Golding over Rousseau any day). It is very difficult to reason morally with children because, well, they are children and have larger concerns than morality – such as their emotional needs and interests.

One can try bargaining. For instance, you can tell a child that if they don't stop hitting the baby with a stick, they will not get a story read to them that night. This doesn't usually stop them hitting the baby. This is because, when it comes to tonight and the reading is withheld, they have entirely forgotten – emotionally if not consciously - what the punishment was for.

Sadly, it seems to be that parents are often thrown back into the temptations of instantaneous punishment – this time, psychological rather than physical. Anger is displayed. Voices are raised. Love is withheld. Disgust is registered. Sarcasm is vented. Instead of physical abuse some form psychological abuse is vented, either mild or severe. Is that so much preferable?

I wish I had a solution to this problem, but I don't. I know that you're meant to be consistent in punishment, but people just aren't. I grab at whatever sanction comes into my head at any given moment of crisis, and I try my best to follow through if it involves a long term injunction (no TV for a week! No puddings for two days!). In the end I am as bad at punishing as my children are at being punished. Amazing, really, that they have turned out to be such lovely kids.

There still remain temptations to smacking – not from me, but my children. My oldest frequently used to urge me to smack her in preference to other punishments ('it's just over so quick') but I can't stand the idea of smacking any more. Anyway if it's that much of a soft option, it probably won't work. Then again, nothing does. Which perfectly sums up the nature of punishment, both in the family and society at large. It's mainly futile – but it's fundamentally inevitable.

WHEN DID PEOPLE START?

One of the most difficult dilemmas you have to face as a parent is the tricky questions children ask. Contrary to my expectations before becoming a father, kids are annoyingly intelligent, and ask things that most adults have long ago stopped asking because of their difficult and controversial nature.

A few you can just Google. 'Why is the Sky Blue?' is not something I ever had a response to until becoming a parent, but now I know that it's because blue light has the shortest wavelength of all the colours and therefore gets scattered in the more easily then the rest when white light, which made up of all the colours, hits the atmosphere. Feel free to write that down.

Others are trickier. 'Which came first, the chicken or the egg?' is still one I tend to deflect since I haven't got a bleeding clue, and it seems to bring into play difficult philosophical questions which I am not equipped to process, still less communicate to a six year old child. So my response is usually one of two a) the chicken or b) the egg. Either way, it usually buys me some time to find a distraction.

Until quite recently Louise, my youngest, has been asking me if I believe in God. This is for the reasons that fundamentalist Christians usually ask the same question, i.e., to browbeat you into agreeing with your point of view. Louise has long been a head-banger for the faith, not quite understanding yet that one only goes to a faith school in order to get better exam results not to actually sign up for a medieval world view.

So I usually tell her that I'm not sure – which of course doesn't satisfy her any more than it would satisfy Billy Graham. The fact that her sister, Eva, told her that Jesus hated her may have shaken her faith, but just last week she told me she didn't believe in God any more but science. That's probably a step in the right direction.

On a more touchy note, and a more serious one, probably the most difficult question any of my daughters every asked me was 'do you still love mummy?' when I was getting divorced from my first wife. There was no proper answer to this. A 'yes' gave them false hope of reconciliation. A 'no' broke their heart. I can't remember what I actually said, because I have blanked the whole period out, but it was almost certainly obfuscation.

Obfuscation is an intrinsic part of dealing with these impossible questions. One that has come from all of my children at one time or another is

'Who do you love best'? To tell them I love them all equally doesn't seem to cut the mustard – they are determined to have a specific individual named, which they always assume will be them, or fear that it won't be. In the end its probably best to refer them to Frankie Boyle's response in the Guardian Questionnaire when asked 'have you ever told anyone you've loved them and not meant it'. His answer was 'only my children'. That usually shuts them up.

It was a JOKE ok, guys. I love you *all* the most, right? Anyway, here are a few other impossible questions. What happens when you die? Probably best to resist the pat response, which is you face oblivion forever and are then eaten by worms. No one over eight buys 'heaven' anymore, so I usually go for 'no-one really knows'. This is rarely satisfactory, and is followed by 'but what do YOU think'. The answer, naturally, is 'heaven'.

A few more to which I'm afraid there is no answer – 'what was that funny noise you were making in the bedroom last night?

Were you hurting mummy?' 'When did people start' and 'why do people have to die'. There is only one response to these, which also works for the other tricky posers. I find it infallible. 'Ask mummy.'

THE SMACK INSIDE

I should probably be regretting the column I wrote two weeks ago about sex. It was too personal, and it embarrassed my wife. One of the things one needs to learn as a writer sometimes is knowing when to shut the fuck up.

On the other hand, I don't really regret it – not because it wasn't probably a mistake, but because I'm not sure regret is much use to anyone about anything. There was a much visited article in the Guardian recently by Susie Steiner called 'Five Regrets of the Dying'. I am pleased to say that I didn't tick any of the five boxes.

My lack of regret is not so much to do with the fact that I haven't made mistakes in my life – I've made mistakes pretty much every day of my life. It's more to do with my belief that regret is not something that happens to you, but something you do to yourself.

It's something we get into the habit of as children - and no doubt teach our children to do the same. If we make a mistake, the emotion of regret is put there - by cultural transmitters like parents and churches - to try and ensure we don't make the same mistake again.

When I was 13 years old, I saved up for months for a table tennis bat that I wanted more than anything in the world. The first day I owned it, I took it on the bus to my local table tennis club. On the way home, I left it on the bus. I was devastated.

When I got home, my parents did not console me. They told me I should learn my lesson, and that I had been a fool and should look after my stuff better. So on top of the grief – it's not too big a word – of losing the bat, I suffered the sense that I was a bad, stupid and inadequate person. They were not cruel parents. They just wanted me to learn not to forget things.

Did it stop me leaving things on buses? No. I remain, more than 40 years later, the sort of person who forgets things on buses and always will be. I continue to lose stuff on a weekly basis. The emotion of deep regret, instilled in as a child, had absolutely no utility.

So the difference when I lose something now is that, although I am unhappy about it, I don't reproach myself. In short, I don't regret it. I try not to regret anything at all – not because I am a psychopath, but because regret serves no purpose.

Regret, and its close relative, shame, are useless, if not harmful, emotions, which I try not to 'do' and which I try not to impose on my children. They strike me as hangovers from our Christian heritage, and are of the same order of the discredited philosophy that we should smack our children when they are naughty.

That smack would always come with a profound sense of reproach attached, so that we could drive home the difference between 'right' and 'wrong'. We have done away with the smacking, but we subtly tried to replace it with the 'inner smack' – to try and make sure that the children punish themselves, without us having to take on the guilt of punishing them as parents.

And it works – up to a point. I still feel an echo of guilt when I lose something important and sometimes shame as well (guilt is "I did something wrong', shame is 'I am something wrong'). But I'm still the same absent-minded schmuck I was when I was a child.

The sense of having done wrong is too deeply embedded in my childhood self to entirely escape, but I have, at least, managed to stop doing the regret. Why? Because it's imaginary interest self-imposed on something you've already paid for.

THE SECRET OF A
SUCCESSFUL MARRIAGE

I would like to write a column about what makes for a successful marriage, which is unfortunate, since I don't know what makes for a successful marriage. All I know is what a working marriage looks like from close up, which is a different thing

The first thing to say about 'happy marriages' is that I doubt that there are very many of them. Half of all people get divorced. I suspect that another half of those remaining are hanging on because of children or money or fear of loneliness.

Of the remaining 25 percent, maybe another half could be called truly and consistently happy, and I expect this is out of a fortunate combination of circumstance rather than any particular brand of love or tactic. Perhaps that portion comprise those lucky people who are just 'made' for marriage, who fit each other in prejudice, affiliation and sentiment and happen to have both been born with cheerful, patient natures

Most of the remaining marriages I think are not about happiness or unhappiness, but accommodation and negotiation. And I say that as half of a married couple in which both of us have probably made one another both happy and unhappy during our relationship, probably in roughly equal measure. We are very different people, but then all people are very different people. And therein lies the central dilemma of marriage which asks you to spend close company with one person for years on end.

My wife and I are both have a very strong sense of individuality and I like that, but it means we have our fair share of fireworks. Anyone who doesn't have a lot of disagreements in a marriage is probably repressing a lot of stuff and which is liable explode sooner or later.

I have already had one marriage that didn't work out (I hesitate to call it a failed marriage because it succeeded for a fair while) and this one has already lasted a lot longer, which I take as a good sign. We have the basics – we love each other – but that is just the beginning. To me there are three keys to marriage and they are all very difficult to forge.

The first is communication, which I have written about here before and which I don't intend to go into again. Suffice to say good communication requires practice, goodwill, determination and a considerable amount of inborn talent.

The second is respect which in many ways is more important than love. Love comes and goes, but respect endures, and provides the space for love to flow after the ebb, which is bound to come in all long marriages sooner or later.

The third is trust. And this is the hardest of all, because if you have ever been let down, and we all have, reconstructing the trust is difficult. This isn't about infidelity but many small matters – broken promises, bad intentions, frustrated hopes.

You have to trust, even though you have no guarantee you wont be let down, and then, if you are let down, trust again, and then again. You must keep doing this as long as you are humanly able, and your marriage either will stand or fall on it.

This requires what I call the power of 'forgettory' as opposed to memory. You need to forget and forget again about any perceived hurts and mistreatment. Dragging the weight of past behind you will drag you down in the end.

But you will never, can never, 'get there' because there is nowhere to get. A marriage is a moving process, a living thing, and if it stops being fed with these existential nutrients, it will finally expire. Complacency and laziness is what kills marriage, far more than lack of love, and that is why it is often described as hard work. But no work is ultimately more rewarding.

SEX

The most repulsive thing I could imagine when I was a teenager was the thought of my parents – or for that matter anyone over 30 – having sex, especially with one another.

Those wrinkled denizens of the latter half of life's journey were deemed beyond the sexual pale. Presumably it happened – occasionally - in theory, but the actual reality was too gross to contemplate.

There was a secondary fear associated with this. I presumed that, as I got older, I would end up long term with someone or other, either in marriage our outside it. The downside of this was the sex would become predictable, safe and ultimately dull, if it continued at all.

These fears turned out to be unfounded. It seems that the flexibility of the human mind has the ability to screen out the imperfections of age, as you age yourself. My wife is twelve years older than when I first saw her, - but she genuinely doesn't appear to me any different. I don't fancy her any less. She may not feel the same about me, but if she has mourned her handsome prince turning into a wizened toad, she has done a good job of concealing the fact.

As for variety, sex turns out to be one of these things that have a strange limitlessness, like music. Every event is a new combination of notes. Sometimes the notes don't make a perfect chord, but its always, somehow, a unique experience.

There's a Zen aspect of older, married sex. In the years after I lost my virginity, I was very conscious of what I was doing even while I was doing it. Now, it is as if the experience is having me rather than the other way round. Some force seems to instruct you. This I know sounds rather esoteric, but it's the only way I can think of to describe the experience. – consciously automatic, in a good way.

This seems to support the old cliché, established no doubt by old people, that sex is better among those in a long established, loving relationship. I'm not so sure that's true. This trope chimes with the idea that sex without love is a meaningless experience, but I am with Woody Allen - 'as meaningless experiences go its still one of the best'. To love someone when you have sex with them is great, but not entirely necessary.

There is a very separate kind of pleasure to be had from the loveless, short-term sex – the joy of discovery, of novelty, of self-affirmation. For me, obviously, it's off the menu – not only on a moral basis, but because sex based on purely physical attraction doesn't usually happen when your body looks more like suet than a six-pack. That doesn't mean the menu doesn't contain delights.

I like married sex though. It tends to be relatively more available, at least after sufficient whining. Secondly you don't have to deal with the fact that, if the person you're sleeping with has only been selected for sex, there's no worry about getting rid of them in the morning. Conversely, you can reasonably expect your sexual partner not to do a runner as soon as she gets a look at your mug in the cold light of day.

There comes a point when some couples feel it's OK to say 'oh I like a nice cup of tea or a game of Scrabble' better than sex. If you get to that stage, in my opinion, your marriage is going tits up, even if you're wife isn't.

Sure, as you get older, it's always more tempting to just go to sleep. But sex, if you can be bothered, is not only better than anything else. - It's the only thing that distinguishes your relationship with your wife from any other person. As such, it is the mark of uniqueness and therefore uniquely precious.

THERE'S NO SUCH THING AS FUN FOR ALL THE FAMILY

One of my favourite Jerry Seinfeld sayings is, "There's no such thing as fun for *all* the family." How true, how brutal, how brutally true. And how topical, given the looming holiday season.

I have seen one too many tube posters featuring mummy, daddy and the little moppets throwing their heads back in laughter as against a photoshopped beach to suppress my gag reflex anymore. It's a swiz.

I have probably been on more than 50 family holidays and I have come to the conclusion that each member of the group tends to subtract from the pleasure of the other. This is a cruel paradox, understandably not mentioned by travel companies – but 'holidays' and 'families' tend to be incompatible, because each member of the group tends to have contradictory aims. The word holiday, from 'holy day' implies a day of rest. Which, as a working definition, is blackly comic.

What I want on a holiday is simple. Firstly, I want to get there and back with the minimum stress. Children agitate against this. They fight with each other in the car. They demand to be entertained on the train. They are sick on the plane. They ask whether or not we are there yet. As a general rule, we are not.

Having endured the journey, what I hope for is a bit of peace and quiet. I want to read the books I've been waiting to read, lob myself like a side of beef onto a sun bed and not have to worry about anything. In the evening I want to have a sumptuous dinner, then I want to fall asleep, slightly drunk, among crisp white sheets.

What my daughters want is different. Primarily, they want to immerse themselves in water. Children love a pool. But they are not content to do fifty lengths and stretch out on the lounger. They want to throw balls to you for hours on end, or play 'here comes the shark' or 'hold your breath' or any of a limitless number of aquatic larks which can exhaust the patience of the most dedicated parent, let alone a 56-year old grouch with a short attention span.

Is that it, when the swimming's over? No it is not. They want you to do other stuff with them. Stuff that they enjoy. Teaching them to play tennis, or Ping-Pong, or beach volleyball, or canoeing. This is fun for them. It is dull for you. And made worse by the fact that you have to strenuously pretend that it isn't dull.

You may try catch a break by taking them to a nice art gallery or going shopping, or visiting museums, but they do not like this. They get bored. They need to be entertained. Given the absence of all their school friends, who exist for this purpose, that task falls to you.

Then there's all the joy of mealtimes. The food may be unfamiliar and the children will insist on eating sort of crap that is publicly embarrassing. I remember going to a 5 star hotel in Mauritius and out of the most amazing buffet I have ever seen in my life, and two of my daughters returning with a few crackers, some butter and a can of coke. It's remarkable how annoying this can be.

I know this must seem curmudgeonly, and it is, and I do actually have very many happy memories of holidays with my family. Walking on the beach with them, watching them play in the sand, flying kites together, searching for crabs for together under distant rocks. Seeing their untrammelled happiness, to be free under open skies, is an incredible gift and privilege to witness.

In fact if you think of it as extended childcare, or a very long and expensive Sunday, or an exercise in bonding, than it's a big success. Just don't confuse it with a holiday, and you won't be disappointed.

SEPARATION ANXIETY

When my eldest daughter, Jean, now eighteen, was five years old I took her to the cinema to see the Disney version of 'The Little Mermaid'. Towards the end, the Mermaid has to say goodbye to her father, so that she can go and live on land with the handsome (human) prince.

At this scene, Jean started to weep. I imagine she was experiencing the premonition that the fairy tale was designed to elicit – the moment of separation between father and daughter.

I think – partly from talking to other fathers – that this is a very particular kind of separation, qualitatively different from separation between fathers and sons, or mothers and children of either gender. The relationship between father and daughter is jealous, passionate, and bears many of the marks of a non-sexual love affair.

Nothing, for me, compares to the unqualified love I receive from my daughters. Even now, when I walk through the door, the youngers ones – 5 and 9 – will often run to me, screaming with excitement and hugging me ecstatically, an a joy which I fully reciprocate. Such passion has only one way to go – downhill, into separation and adulthood.

The loss does not happen overnight. It begins when the daughter no longer wants you to read to her in bed anymore. Then they don't want to go to the playground anymore. Then – perhaps the hardest blow – they get a boyfriend, their Human Prince, to supplant you, the King of the Ocean.

I recall going to see Jean in a play a few years back, and her coming down the stairs in triumph after her brilliant performance. I waited for her to come to me, as I stood there, beaming all over my face. She ran instead to a young man to the side of the steps. It was her Prince.

One can console oneself that it is not the losing of love, but its transformation. But sometimes that is hard to continue to believe, the process of necessary separation from one's father – or in fact either parent – involves hostility.

I have been very aware over the last five years that what was the purest love I ever knew has turned to skepticism, resentment, sometimes even hatred. I know as a father I should be able to absorb such things - man up! – but the mourning countenance of the Ocean King cannot always be held at bay.

Jean is at university now. She was back for her Easter break for a month, during which we saw each other three times in total. The second time, the argument was so bad, she didn't come back again. She doesn't run to the door to greet me any more. She runs out the door to escape me.

I know we have special issues. Jean is my daughter from my first marriage, and she has found the transition to a 'melded family' a difficult one. All children blame their parents – I still blame my father for stuff I should have shouldered responsibility for long ago. And thus I am the progenitor of her pain, of her perceived exclusion from the 'second family', of her status as the product of a 'broken home'.

Her pain is not the sad, knowing pain of the Little Princess. It is an inchoate fury, which scatters debris over everything in its path – not just me, but her sisters, who feel her loss just as I do.

One day, I know, we will be able to stand in a room together without hurling insults at one another. One day, I know, we will be good friends. One day, I know, the family will stand together again. But the Little Mermaid has left the sea for the land. And the King of Ocean watches, mutely, as distant waves gather, welling out of the deep.

MALE VANITY

You probably haven't noticed that the photo of the weird gimpy looking chap at the top of this column has been replaced by a slightly different photo of the same weird gimpy looking chap. It has changed for a very shallow reason - because I didn't like the old one.

You probably haven't noticed because you couldn't care less. Which is the tragedy of all vanity, but particularly male vanity. Female vanity has a hinterland of purposefulness. Watch any make-over programme and you can see that any dried up old biscuit can be transformed, by a few clever strokes of make up and hair dye, and snips of scissors, and cuts of cloth, into ravishing cheesecake.

Do the same to a man however, and he's likely to remain looking pretty much like he did before, lacking the props of cosmetics, big hair, heels and couture dresses. He may polish up nicely. He may have a nicer suit on and a better haircut. But it's the same cut of meat.

Female vanity is normalized in a way that male vanity is not. My ten-year-old daughter has just had her ears pierced. My 5-year-old loves to put on the slap. To concentrate on your appearance as a woman is (unlike in the DM and boiler suited 1980s) considered a bold stroke of reinvention and power. For a man it simply poncing about. Which is pretty much how my wife sees it when I disport myself in front of a mirror every morning.

For I am a vain man – of a particular type. Not is the kind who genuinely thinks he's gorgeous and admires his reflection as a manifestation of natural beauty to be appreciated like a rose or a sunset. I am the other, more common variety – the kind who always feels that he is, through clothes and grooming, trying to compensate for a perceived lack of natural allure.

When I look in the mirror adjusting my wardrobe, I am seeking to compensate for the scars on my face and body (I have seven in all, including a repaired cleft lip), my lack of stature - I am slightly over 5'6") (note that poignant 'slightly over') and my all round lack of symmetry (one eyelid lower than the other, one foot larger than the other) As I grow older, my lack of hair, surfeit of wrinkles and embarrassment of waistline are added to the aesthetic burden.

My vanity grows, not shrinks as I age – that is, I feel more and more compelled to take steps to compensate for the ruin of my body and face. As my wife looks on, suppressing smirks, I change my shirt for a third time until it sits nicely with my expensive jeans. Meanwhile it remains permitted to say to a man, 'you are looking old/porky/crap' in a way that one could never do to a wife or a daughter.

Thus vanity feeds on vanity, and insecurity on insecurity. Like those old gentlemen of an earlier generation, who dress up in a suit and tie every day long after they have a place of work to go to, men like me try to preserve their dignity by buffing their personal appearance. A woman is expected to do such things. A man, and particularly a husband, is mocked for it – and yet equally derided for 'letting himself go'.

I deeply wish I could be rid of vanity – as I'm sure many women wish they could be rid of theirs. I want the mirror to reflect the elegance of the inside of my head, the flair of my imagination, the dignity of my intelligence. Instead it insists on reflecting my body, and all the disappointments encapsulated there. This, I dare say, is how it feels to be a woman. Nowadays, men feel it too, but do not talk of it. Because for males, the love that dare not speak its name is no longer homosexuality. It is vanity.

HOW TO BE VULNERABLE

I attended a lecture by a fascinating character last week – Brenee Brown, whose TED talk 'On Vulnerability' on the web has so far produced 6 million hits. I can see why it's so popular. Brown discusses a neglected subject - the importance of vulnerability in healthy adults, and how we need to teach it to our children.

This seems a strange thing to suggest – since what is more vulnerable than a child? A parent can crush their children with a word, a gesture, or even a facial expression.

And yet the path to adulthood – Brown points out – includes building defences against vulnerability. Boys learn that they must not fall off their white charger – they must be strong, compete in the workplace and not show inappropriate emotion. Girls, too, often grow into women who feel they must at all costs cope with anything the world throws at them, hating to ask for help.

The only alternative to vulnerability is to numb yourself. Oddly enough, this is a perception I had at a very young age – maybe as young as 14 – and have held to ever since. If you want pleasure, you have to feel pain. Those who deny their vulnerability try to have their cake and eat it. What they end up with is a very stale cake.

How can you get your children to protect the vulnerability that they are born with? Some people do, of course, and these are the people that Brown describes as 'wholehearted'. They come from a place that is not artificial – it includes all their fears and insecurities as well.

The people who are not wholehearted are – obviously – capable of fear and insecurity as well (only sociopaths aren't). They just don't recognize or acknowledge their vulnerability, and tuck that part of themselves away – sometimes quite literally, obsessively tidying the external world to keep chaos at bay.

They aim for perfection, and see themselves as capable of it. When things go wrong, they tend to blame other people rather than themselves, or blame themselves unduly. They also tend to make everything uncertain, certain – 'I'm right, you're wrong, shut up.'

Brown recognises this not only from study but from experience – when she was forced to face her own vulnerability, during her research work, she had a nervous breakdown.

How can I teach my four daughters to see their vulnerability as not shameful? One way is accepting their imperfection. Brown says, "You see this perfect baby, and say 'I must keep her perfect'. So that she goes to Yale or he makes the football team. But that's not our job as parents. Our job is to say 'you are imperfect, but you are worthy of love and belonging'.

It all sounds a bit American self-helpy, and it is, but in a good sense, since it is wise and thoughtful. When I was a child, I learned that it was babyish to cry, or unmanly, and so I defined my vulnerability it as weakness. But it isn't. Brown demonstrates this in her TED talk. She asks the audience whether they think vulnerability equates with weakness. Most put their hands up. Then she asks if they thought it was brave of her to stand up and admit she had had a nervous breakdown. All the hands went up.

This makes the point perfectly. To be vulnerable is to be strong, because you are strong enough to face up to what all human beings intrinsically are – flawed and somewhat raw. We live in a vulnerable world, and there is no escaping it.

This is what living with vulnerability means – risking it. "We must let ourselves be seen, deeply seen, vulnerably seen" says Brown. For to be vulnerable is to know we are alive. Children know that from the off. We must protect them from having that stolen - by allowing them to feel, and by allowing them to fail.

HOW TO BE VULNERABLE 2

When I was growing up, never once did I witness my parents have a fight, or exchange a cross word. I never even saw either my mother or father visibly sad or upset. Adult emotions stayed hidden.

I have been inclined to apply these same principles in front of my own children. My disagreements with my wife, my upsets and private griefs, have tended to stay behind closed doors

It always seemed to me that Jean, Rose, Louise and Eva are privileged by witnessing a theatrical performance rather than documentary reality. Rose, who is 20, declines to read my very personal memoir 'The Scent of Dried Roses' because she doesn't want her image of me compromised.

For reasons of vanity, I, too, would rather be the person she fantasises me to be rather than the desperate, frightened person I portray myself as in that book. Although the events took place 25 years ago, Ruby doesn't feel ready to assimilate that aspect of my past. That is her right and her choice.

Similarly, my wife and I have both recently lost our fathers. I have kept a stiff upper lip, (my wife has been more visibly upset). My daughter, Lydia, states emphatically that she hates to see either of us cry. Jean was thankful that I had kept my grief in check at my father's funeral.

Yet recently, I have begun to question this airbrush parenting – through conversations with social researcher Brenee Brown, whose TED talk, 'On Vulnerability' has now received nearly 10 million hits. I have written about Brenee before in this column after watching that lecture. Last week I interviewed her and she raised a lot of questions over my ideal of being a 'strong father' for my children.

She pointed out that children do not learn from what you tell them. Simply telling your children that its 'OK to be vulnerable' doesn't work. They learn from how you model yourself. You can't have healthy children unless those children see healthy parents.

Brenee uses the word 'wholehearted' to indicate those people who are secure enough to both experience and demonstrate their vulnerability, rather than numb themselves to feeling or keep their emotions hidden. Wholehearted people, since they are on terms with negative feelings, tend not to experience shame at their reactions to loss, failure or disappointment. That feeling of shame comes as a result of learning in early life to interpret vulnerability as weakness.

People presented with the model as a child that I was shown by my 'perfect parents' might well come to the belief, for instance, that a marriage which suffered conflict was somehow not worth the effort – which, she said, emphatically, was 'the biggest load of crap I've heard in my life.'

Disagreement is normal and should be shown as such. She chooses not to hide her conflicts with her husband, Steve, in front of their two children, who are seven and 14 years old. She says she 'tries to normalize that relationships are tough"

So if it's healthy to model conflict in front of your children, is it also OK to cry in front of them? I asked her if she were to experience violent grief whether she would just go into the next room to avoid her children seeing her upset. She would not.

This all feels somewhat counterintuitive – certainly for fathers, who, are conventionally expected to 'hang tough' when things get rocky. But she insists this is not a matter or opinion but an empirical conclusion borne of years of careful and thorough research.

I find such a view reassuring for parents, many of whom, like me, must spend a lot of time editing themselves for the purposes of 'saving' their children. But with the best of intentions we may be condemning them to something worse than momentary upset – a future tainted by shame, and an unrealistic vision of what adult relationships look like.

WAYS OF ANNOYING WOMEN

I am in dereliction of duty. This column is called 'In the Company of Women' and I have written thus far almost entirely about my daughters. There is a simple, ignoble, reason for this. I am scared of pissing women off.

I have a knack for annoying women. As a result, I try not to make any observations about women in general. Making observations about women in general is one of the things that annoy women in general.

Should I have the recklessness to step over this hurdle, I am likely to find myself in deeper water, by attempting to define them against men. If I suggest 'they' are different from men, this irritates one constituency, the humanist 'we're all the same only culture makes us different' camp. To point out that even if culture makes us different, it still makes us different, is to invite additional calumny.

'Women and men are basically the same' is a statement that may go down well, since it avoids all kinds of tricky areas. Unfortunately, this seems to me to fly in the face of an awful lot of empirical truths - most obviously in the huge range of very different kind of media and consumer products men and women continue to purchase 50 years after second wave feminism started to modify gender roles.

Suggesting that women are superior to men will buy you credit with a certain constituency, but more often than not women like to pretend that they are not superior to men – although I suspect this is sometimes false modesty. I remember a conversation with a group of successful career women who insisted to me passionately that women were not in any way superior to men, it was just that men were differently-abled.

I asked them what made women different. They listed a catalogue of fairly uncontroversial characteristics – women were more nurturing, intuitive, communicative, sociable, emotionally intelligent etc. I then asked them what made men different. Um, they were *less* intuitive communicative, sociable, etc. Apparently we weren't equally abled after all.

Suggesting that women are inferior to men, which is basically my position, is less popular but more easily provably by their historically less successful performances in the workplace, politics, business, comedy, sport, science, art, classical music, war and crossword puzzles.

Whoa. Just joking there. Actually I just wanted to see how it felt to write those words (rather bracing, as a matter of fact.) Obviously I am aware of the patriarchy skewing the playing field, both historically and presently. All the same, with the expression of those few satirical sentences, I probably did enough to raise the ire of yet another group of women, i.e., those who consider jokes concerning the oppression of their gender as being in de facto poor taste.

This is just the conceptual stuff. There are many more practical ways of annoying women. Not doing household chores is one of them, of course, but doing them is also irritating, since they rarely come up to the standard demanded, and doing them too well is humiliating. Being a new man is good – sensitive, listening, caring – but being too unmanly, i.e. submissive, body conscious or vain, is also annoying for women. Dominant sexual behaviour can be good, but on some days it's very, very annoying, if not outright bad. Being rich is good, being materialistic is annoying. And so on.

Just to sum up, in order not to annoy women, you must not suggest that all women are different, or the same, or better. Never suggest they are inferior even in areas where they clearly are, like weightlifting or writing 'best film' lists. Do the household chores, don't do the household chores, be masterful or sensitive, it's all the same in the end as far as women are concerned - annoying. Because women after all are, you know. Women. With exceptions, obviously. Or not. Perhaps.

DODGING COMMUNICATION

It's often said that communication is the secret of a successful marriage. This is rather akin to say that peace is the solution to war. It's true, but there's not much use in saying so.

I am fascinated by our human determination to not communicate. We are extraordinarily good at not hearing what we want to hear and not saying what we need to say. And nowhere do we fail to communicate more effectively than within the confines of an intimate relationship.

Just in case any of you struggle with this important tool for maintaining unhappy unions, I would like to share with you my point-by-point guide to How Not To Communicate. Once you have mastered this you will never again have struggle with uncomfortable thoughts about how other people's views fail to reflect yours sufficiently, or how to cope with having your ego punctured by the cheap shot of an accurate observation or an honest remark.

If someone is talking too much sense in your direction – interrupt them. This will have the dual utility of annoying them and preventing them completing a train of logic that might not be welcome in your particular freight yard.

If this strategy fails, don't worry – there are many other ways of not communicating. Pretend not to hear. Shout. Say the other person is 'boring you'. Suddenly remember an important phone call. 'Realise' that you're too busy to be having this conversation. Find some irrelevant channel of the discussion and sail off down it. If the other person gets emotional, even slightly, refuse to talk to someone who is losing their temper. If they stay calm, say they are patronizing you.

What should you do in an emergency? Let's say, in a moment of sheer recklessness, you mistakenly concede ground and admit that the other person might have a point. Don't panic. It's not the end of the world.

Next time the subject comes up just pretend it never happened. Or, if you are tricked into admitting that some kind of meaningful discussion really did take place, simply misremember it, so that it appears that the ground you have given up has not been conceded at all.

Sometimes, deep in the night, you might wake and ask yourself - what's the point of all these evasions, and digressions, and frantic strategies of self-defence? Wouldn't it be better to listen to the still small voice that tells you that although communication is painful and frightening it is the only way for a relationship to thrive?

When that voice comes, I strongly advise you to SHUT IT OUT. Otherwise, before you know it, important things you believe about your relationship and yourself might start to come unraveled, and you might have to make a painful effort to redraw your world view – without you quite so squarely at the centre of it.

So, be vigilant and be aware. And if the worst comes to the worst, just end the relationship. Then you'll never have to listen to your partner again, and you worldview will be secure. You'll have won the argument. And that's the most important thing. Right?

WHAT MEN TALK ABOUT WHEN WOMEN AREN'T LISTENING

I'm going to stick my trembling head above the parapet this week and reveal what men secretly talk about when the women aren't around – at least the men I've known over the last 20 or so years.

Contrary to myth, they hardly ever talk about sex. They almost never bitch about other men. They do talk about football, music, films, TV and politics. They do value humor highly. They banter, josh and wind up. And sometimes they talk about their marriages.

Some men are genuinely happy in the marriages and don't have much to say. Others are reluctant to speak out. But many are frustrated. None of these men are cavemen. Most of them are fully signed up to feminism in one form or another. Yet the same issues crop up time and again.

Those dissatisfactions in full:

1. *Credit.* Husbands* with children feel they don't get enough credit from their wives. This is especially true when the man is the main wage earner. Going to work every day and taking financial responsibility tends to be seen as a privilege, an 'escape' from childcare. But like childcare itself, a 9-5 job can be both a privilege and a burden.

2. *Respect.* Husbands sometimes feel they don't get enough respect from their wives - who stereotype their husbands as childish

and failing to address their responsibilities properly. Men are infan-tilized. But perhaps men are just living up to expectations.

3. *Priorities* – men are a low priority for their wives, compared with work, children, friends etc. I once asked my wife to draw up a list of her life priorities. I think I scraped in at about fourth.

Please, skeptical women readers, whose lips I can sense collec-tively curling, don't write in with comments like 'diiddums' and 'Well it's your turn to feel like that after six centuries'. It's crass and dull. Children need fathers, as well as mothers, that they can look up to.

Perhaps wives would also feel better if they respected their hus-bands more. I have mentioned previously that I attended a mar-riage course last year. They taught a very shocking thing. – that you should put your partner first. Not your children or your work or your friends.

To a lot of women that is a copout, a throwback to the 1950s. But wouldn't they expect to be put first? Yet this expectation can be a one-way street. To many modern women, a man is seen as ultimately dispensable. Perhaps he is. But you can't expect any man to welcome the news.

It is easy to sideline these observations as whining. But perhaps that's just a way of not facing reality. Fifty years of feminism has meant that the grievances of the wife are sanctified in the way that the grievances of a husband are not. If a woman has a problem, it tends to be taken seriously. If a man has a problem, it tends to be waved away or patronized out of existence.

(Or so men tell me. So don't shoot the messenger. Anyway, this isn't a story about 'women' but people in long-term relationships.)

I emailed this article to half a dozen mates to make sure no-one felt I was speaking out of turn. No one did. The replies I got were not angry. They were moving and rather sad. Many men nowadays don't on the whole feel great about themselves. Men suffer low self-esteem just as much as women do.

Wives can choose to listen or not. All I can note is that in all the relationships I've seen die over the last ten years, it's always been the man that bolts. Perhaps it's that allegedly intractable male vice of irresponsibility. Or perhaps there are actually valid reasons that the refractions of gender politics renders invisible - and the willful blindness only become apparent when it's too late.

*This refers to any man living in a long-term relationship, married or not.

Printed in Great Britain
by Amazon.co.uk, Ltd.,
Marston Gate.